REPUBLIC THEATRE

42nd Street, West of Broadway

OLIVER D. BAILEY — John Yorke, Manager — Sole Lessee

URBAN LEAGUE NIGHT
TUESDAY EVENING, MARCH 27th, 1928

THE THEATRE GUILD
Presents

PORGY

A FOLK PLAY

by

DOROTHY and DuBOSE HEYWARD

The production directed by Rouben Mamoulian
Settings by Cleon Throckmorton

CHARACTERS
(In the order of appearance)

MARIA, keeper of the cookshop	GEORGETTE HARVEY
JAKE, Clara's husband	WESLEY HILL
LILY	DOROTHY PAUL
MINGO	RICHARD HUEY
ANNIE	ELLA MADISON
SPORTING LIFE	PERCY VERWAYNE
SERENA, Robbin's wife	ROSE McCLENDON
ROBBINS, a young stevedore	LLOYD GRAY
JIM, a stevedore	PETER CLARK
CLARA, Jake's wife	MARIE YOUNG
PETER, the honeyman	HAYES PRYOR
PORGY, a crippled beggar	FRANK WILSON
CROWN, a stevedore	PAUL ROBESON
CROWN'S BESS	EVELYN ELLIS
A DETECTIVE	STANLEY DE WOLFE
TWO POLICEMEN	HUGH RENNIE, EDWARD HARTFORD
UNDERTAKER	LEIGH WHIPPER
SCIPIO	MELVILLE GREENE
SIMON FRAZIER, a lawyer	A. B. COMATHIERE
NELSON, a fisherman	J. EDWARD BROWN
ALAN ARCHDALE	EDWARD FIELDING
THE CRAB MAN	LEIGH WHIPPER
THE CORONER	GARRETT MINTURN

RESIDENTS OF CATFISH ROW, FISHERMEN, CHILDREN, STEVEDORES, etc.—
Clarissa Bley, Marguerite Booth, Lillian Cowan, Catherine Francis, Ella Gordon, Rose Johnson, Marie Mason, Dorothy West, Moss Williams, Thomas Allen, Maurice Green, Richard Huey, Edward Chezzer, Edward Charles, A. B. DeComathiere, Stanley De Wolfe, Philip Thomas
CHILDREN—Eddie Williams, Ruth Williams, Emmie Bellman, Elycia Harrigan, William Carroll, Martha Donaldson
JENKINS' ORPHANAGE BAND—A. J. Mills, Jesse Coon, John Wilson, Arthur Kennedy, Thaddeus Jenkins, Lester Hubbard, Walter Brooks, Samuel Ladson, Alexa Mills, Jr., Lewis Johnson, Frank Smith.

SYNOPSIS OF SCENES

ACT I.
Scene 1—Catfish Row. A Summer evening.
Scene 2—Serena's Room. The Following Night.

ACT II.
Scene 1—Catfish Row. A Month Later.
Scene 2—A Palmetto Jungle. Evening the Same Day.
Scene 3—Catfish Row. Before Dawn. A Week Later.
Scene 4—Serena's Room. Dawn of the Following Day.
(Intermission Twelve Minutes)

ACT III.
Scene 1—Catfish Row. The Next Night.
Scene 2—Catfish Row. Early Morning.
Scene 3—Catfish Row. Five Days Later.

PLACE—Charleston, S. C.   TIME—The Present.
The bells preceding the act curtains are intended to represent the bells in the clock tower of St. Michael's Church near the Negro quarter of Charleston.

MANAGER — B. M. HUGHES
STAGE MANAGER — Edward Hartford
ASSISTANTS — BARBARA BRUCE, CHERYL CRAWFORD, HUGH RENNIE

NOTES ON PORGY

The band which appears in the third and fourth scenes of the play has been brought to New York for this production. It is the original band of the Jenkins Orphanage in Charleston, and is a part of the musical aggregation described in the large portion of Mr. Heyward's novel. Anyone interested in assisting this Southern Negro orphanage can communicate with them through the office of the Theatre Guild.
For assistance in securing and recording the spirituals used in the play, grateful acknowledgment is made to the Society for the Preservation of Spirituals in Charleston, and to Miss Nan Bagby Stephens.
The dialect employed by the Negroes of the South Carolina Low Country is known as "Gullah." It is so obscure and contains so many words of African origin that, in order to render the dialogue comprehensible, it has been translated into conventional Negro dialect retaining only certain characteristic grammatical eccentricities. The word "Buckra" means a white man, and "Shouting" means the bodily rhythms that accompany the music.

THE THEATRE GUILD, INC.
Board of Managers
Theresa Helburn   Philip Moeller   Maurice Wertheim
Lawrence Langner   Lee Simonson   Helen Westley

Executive Director: Theresa Helburn

Business Manager   Press Department
Warren P. Munsell   Robert F. Sisk

Play Reading Department
Courtenay Lemon

Anita Block, Reader of Foreign Plays

Technical Director   Counsel   Subscription Secretary
Kate Lawson   Charles A. Riegelman   Addie Williams

Address communications to the THEATRE GUILD, INC.
245 West 52nd Street, New York City

LEGACY

TREASURES OF
BLACK

EDITED BY THOMAS C. BATTLE
MOORLAND-SPINGARN
PREFACE BY JOHN HOPE

HISTORY

AND DONNA M. WELLS, RESEARCH CENTER FRANKLIN

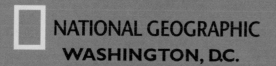
NATIONAL GEOGRAPHIC
WASHINGTON, D.C.

CONTENTS

THE BULL-DOGGER MOVIE POSTER, 1923. Western featuring rodeo star Bill Pickett with an all-Black cast. Omnium Gatherum Collection.

PREFACE

JOHN HOPE FRANKLIN

I WAS IN MY SECOND YEAR as professor at Howard University in 1948 when Arthur Spingarn presented his valuable collection of books, manuscripts, and memorabilia to the university library. His generous gift was combined with material already in the keeping of the library, which had been donated by Jesse Moorland, a distinguished YMCA administrator and longtime friend of Howard. From then on, that part of the library would be known as the Moorland-Spingarn Collection, named for the donors.

The transfer of the materials from Spingarn was a grand occasion. President Mordecai Johnson and other administrators were present, as were several notable university scholars. I went with Rayford Logan, head of the Department of History and already a dear friend and mentor. Dorothy Porter, curator of special collections, presided, and President Johnson spoke especially of the thoughtful generosity of Arthur Spingarn in transferring his valuable collection to Howard University.

Having already become acquainted with the role of the Spingarn family in founding the National Association for the Advancement of Colored People, I was honored to be introduced to Arthur Spingarn and his wife. His brother, Joel, a Columbia University English professor, had been the founding president of the NAACP. Arthur was the legal counsel for the fledgling organization and was instrumental in overthrowing the so-called white primary that prevailed in many parts of the South—the practice of allowing only white voters to participate in primary elections, thus choosing candidates without any participation by African Americans, even though they had the right to vote. Spingarn overturned the white primary when he won the case of *Guinn* v. *United States* in 1915.

I immediately struck up a friendship with Arthur Spingarn, whom I saw subsequently in New York and Washington. Years later, when I was Pitt Professor at Cambridge University and Arthur was visiting in London, I invited him to Cambridge. He readily accepted. This was an occasion for my wife and me to host a grand reception in his honor, and he was delighted to meet our Cambridge friends. On that occasion, perhaps the last time I saw him, he once again remarked on how pleased he was to have a collection bearing his name housed at Howard University, and how he continued to acquire materials to add to the collection. I expressed my pleasure that he had done so, reflecting on the many uses I had made of the materials from the time he placed them there in 1948.

Many thousands have benefited from those materials since, and continue to do so. With this book, the riches of interest and information of the Moorland-Spingarn Collection are now brought to a larger public, in keeping with Arthur Spingarn's original intention to share all the materials of African-American culture and history that he had collected with all those who would take an interest in them.

EDITORS' INTRODUCTION

THOMAS C. BATTLE AND DONNA M. WELLS

KUDUO URN, Ghana, 18th-19th century. Bronze gold dust container. Franklin H. Williams Collection.

Legacy: Treasures of Black History *is a celebration of the work of the Moorland-Spingarn Research Center at Howard University. Since its inception, Moorland's four research divisions have followed a mandate to document the Black experience on a global level through a variety of mediums.*

The Library Division contains more than 200,000 bound volumes; 1,900 serials; 14,000 microfilm reels of newspapers; and an extensive subject, biographical, and local history vertical file. The Howard University Archives maintains 9,157 linear feet of official administrative files and archival files on university units, subjects, and persons; 6,500 theses; 2,400 dissertations; more than 52,000 photographs; 1,050 audiovisual records; and 910 videotapes of events in the arts and humanities. The Manuscript Division houses more than 650 collections of individuals, organizations, and institutions; 1,000 single manuscripts; more than 1,000 oral histories; 15,000 sound recordings; 3,000 pieces of sheet music; and about 100,600 graphic items. The Howard University Museum is both a viewing facility and a central storage facility for 2,500 extremely rare artifacts and three-dimensional items. Highlights include a Babylonian cuneiform and Charles Drew's Spingarn Medal, which was carried into outer space by his nephew, astronaut Frederick Drew Gregory. In 12 thematic chapters Legacy demonstrates the place and use of these treasures in telling the story of the Black experience. The two essays appearing in each chapter provide a historical setting to help understand the context in which the writings, quotes, images, documents, and artifacts used throughout this book were created. Following is an excerpt of a history of Moorland written by its director and Legacy co-author, Thomas C. Battle. The full article is available from Library Quarterly, *vol. 58, no. 2, pp. 143-163.*

SINCE ITS FORMATIVE YEARS, Howard University has collected materials documenting the historical experiences of people of African descent. Gen. Oliver Otis Howard, the founder for whom the institution was named and who was its third president, was an early supporter of the library's development. In April 1867, shortly after the university was chartered, a committee was established to select books for a library. Some of the first books were titles on Africa, and General Howard donated several books and photographs related to

Blacks. Other individuals contributed books dealing with the abolitionist movement and the Civil War. Chief among these donations, and the university's most significant acquisition prior to the formal establishment of a special Black history collection, was the 1873 bequest of Lewis Tappan, a noted abolitionist who had organized the American and Foreign Anti-Slavery Society and served as treasurer of the American Missionary Association. Tappan's Antislavery Collection consisted of more than 1,600 books, pamphlets, newspapers, letters, pictures, clippings, and periodicals.

The Black history collection grew slowly during the 19th century. However, the founding of organizations like the Bethel Literary and Historical Association (1881), the Negro Society for Historical Research (1912), and the Association for the Study of Negro Life and History (1915) was reflective of and stimulated a growing interest in studying and collecting sources for Black history. The university's leading proponent of a separate research collection on Black history was Kelly Miller, a professor of mathematics and sociology (1890-1934) and dean of the College of Arts and Sciences (1907-19). Envisioning a national "Negro Americana Museum and Library," Miller persuaded his good friend, the Reverend Jesse E. Moorland, to donate his private library on Black history to the university for this purpose.

Moorland noted that he was "giving this collection to the University because it is the one place in America where the largest and best library on this subject [of the Negro and slavery] should be constructively established." With this auspicious beginning, Howard University moved to the forefront of institutions documenting Black history and culture.

A new era began for Moorland in 1930 with the appointment of Dorothy Burnett Porter and continued in 1932, when the Moorland Foundation was established as a research library. Over the next 43 years, she devoted herself to developing a modern research library to serve the needs of the university community, as well as an international community of scholars. She greatly augmented the collection's holdings, and the opening of the Founder's Library in 1939 made substantial expansion possible.

A landmark in the Moorland Foundation's history was the purchase in 1946 of the private library of learned bibliophile Arthur Barnette Spingarn. Spingarn was an attorney who chaired the NAACP's legal committee for many years and served as the association's president. He was a widely read scholar of Black history and literature. The acquisition of the Arthur B. Spingarn Collection of Negro Authors combined with Howard's earlier holdings to make the Moorland Foundation "the largest and the most valuable research library in America for the study of Negro life and history."

The collection is particularly strong in its coverage of Afro-Cuban, Afro-Brazilian, and Haitian writers and contains many rare editions. Probably the most famous of these is Juan Latino's *Ad Catholicum Pariter et Invictissimum Philippum dei Gratia Hispaniarum Regum*, published in 1573 at Granada, Spain. It is a volume of epigrams depicting King Philip's victory over the Turks and was written by a Black slave who was one of the outstanding Latinists and humanists of Renaissance Spain and a noted professor at the University of Granada. Indeed, a major feature of the Spingarn Collection is the large number of African writers whose works are represented and who remain largely unknown to American scholars, as well as the works of people of African descent in the Caribbean and Central and South America. The collection is particularly important for its works by early Black American writers

ASHANTI GOLD WEIGHT, Ghana, 18th-19th century. Cast bronze. Franklin H. Williams Collection.

and leaders, including Benjamin Banneker, Richard Allen, David Ruggles, Absalom Jones, and David Walker. In the years after its initial purchase, Spingarn added hundreds of volumes, and the collection grew to contain items in many African languages, such as Swahili, Amharic, Hausa, and Xhosa.

The Moorland general collection has the distinction of housing the earliest imprint, Nicolas Durand de Villegagnon's *Caroli. V. Imperatioris Expeditio in African and Argieram* (1542). Together, the two collections present evidence that should have made notions of Black intellectual inferiority and of pseudoscientific racism clearly unfounded. By 1957, the Moorland Foundation's collections had grown from 3,000 to some 40,000 volumes. In 1957, Moorland acquired Spingarn's collection of Negro music, at the time one of the largest such collections in the world. It included works by Will Marion Cook, Samuel Coleridge-Taylor, Clarence Cameron White, W. C. Handy, Cole and Johnson, Williams and Walker, and Sissle and Blake. Foreign composers represented are José Mauricio Nunes Garcia, regarded as the father of Brazilian music; Justin Elie, Haitian composer of salon music; Amadeo Roldan of Cuba; and world-renowned French violinist Joseph Boulogne, Le Chevalier de Saint-George.

The year 1973 marked the beginning of a new phase of development. Porter retired in June and the new head of the collection assumed leadership. Thus the Moorland-Spingarn Research Center (MSRC) was created; it comprised the existing Jesse E. Moorland and Arthur B. Spingarn Collections, as well as the Howard University Museum, the Howard University Archives, the Black Press Archives, and the Ralph J. Bunche Oral History Collection. Michael Winston, historian alumnus (1962) and former director of research in the History Department, was appointed. While administrative and physical changes were significant, it was the new documentation and research program articulated by Winston that was to have the greatest impact on the center over the next decade. In 1933, Dorothy B. Porter had described the purposes of the Moorland Foundation as: (1) to accumulate, record, and preserve material by and about the Negro, (2) to assist interested students of Negro life to pursue the scholarly exploitation of the material in the collection, (3) to instill race pride and race consciousness in Negro youth, and (4) to provide a great reference library on every phase of Negro life.

While these basic objectives continued to be the foundation of the center's program, the reorganization resulted in a redefinition of approaches to documentation and research. This is best reflected in the creation of a separate Manuscript Division, described by Winston as designed to permit MSRC's development into a thoroughly modern, professional research organization that would produce research in addition to carrying out traditional curatorial and library functions. The division would pursue the programmatic, analytical collecting of documentary sources that would

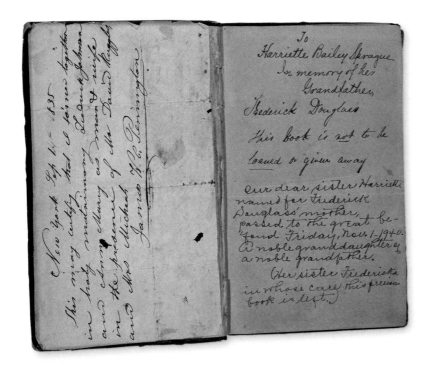

LIFE AND TIMES OF FREDERICK DOUGLASS, by Frederick Douglass, 1881. Contains marriage license of Frederick Johnson (Douglass) and Anna Murray, 1835. Handed down to granddaughter Harriet Bailey Sprague. Library Collection.

enable scholars to probe more deeply beneath the deceptively simple surfaces of Black history and culture. During the reorganization, plans were made to divide the Manuscript Division into four constituent departments: Manuscript, Music, Oral History, and Prints and Photographs. Since 1974, a major acquisitions program has been aggressively pursued, resulting in a tremendous increase in the division's holdings and a growth more rapid than that of any other unit of the MSRC. The division now houses, for example, the papers of Paul Robeson, Vernon Jordan, Charles C. Diggs, Jr., Max Yergan, the Congressional Black Caucus, Mordecai Wyatt Johnson, Benjamin E. Mays, George B. Murphy, Jr., Charles H. Houston, the *Afro-American* series of newspapers, Charles Drew, Ernest E. Just, Mary

Frances Berry, Rayford Logan, the Ancient Egyptian Arabic Order Nobles of the Mystic Shrine, and the law firm of Cobb, Howard, Hayes and Windsor. Coupled with such earlier acquisitions as the papers of Alain Locke and E. Franklin Frazier, the Manuscript Division is now the largest and most diverse repository of primary research materials documenting the Black experience in America.

The new Howard University Museum (HUM) stemmed from Kelly Miller's proposal, made at the time the Moorland Foundation was established. The founders of the university had established a museum as part of the first library as early as 1868. However, its development was apparently abandoned in the early decades of the university's growth. The project remained dormant until the creation of the MSRC in 1973. HUM, which opened in February 1979, is seen primarily as a teaching museum, emphasizing the visual documentation of African and Afro-American history and culture and serving as a resource for formal university instruction as well as a facility available to the public schools and the general community.

Meanwhile, the Library Division continues to augment its holdings. In addition to many other donations and purchases, the MSRC acquired in 1975 the library and papers of alumnus C. Glenn Carrington; this collection resulted from 50 years of great effort and personal sacrifice. As a library collection, it is second only to the Spingarn Collection in size and scope and, at the time of its acquisition, was exceeded only by the Locke Collection in its comprehensiveness. The Carrington Collection contains more than 2,200 books in 15 languages, approximately 500 recordings, and 18 storage boxes of manuscript materials, photographs, broadsides, prints, periodicals, sheet music, newspapers, and a variety of other items. Currently, the MSRC continues to host thousands of scholars and other visitors from many parts of the world. It cooperates with many institutions, individuals, and organizations on publications, exhibitions, and video programs.

MARY CHURCH TERRELL AT CHRISTENING, SIX MONTHS OLD, photographer unknown, 1865. Ambrotype housed in Union case. Mary Church Terrell Papers.

(FOLLOWING PAGES) FIRE!! DEVOTED TO YOUNGER NEGRO ARTISTS, edited by Wallace Thurman, vol. 1, no. 1, November 26, 1926, autographed by contributors. Alain Locke Papers.

Come on Brother, lets go 'round de wall
And dat suits me
Come on Brother, lets go 'round de wall
And dat suits me
Come on Brother lets go 'round de wall
Don't wanta stumble and Ah don't wanta fall
And it's a no hindering cause
And dat suits me

Zora Neale Hurston

FIRE!!

DEVOTED TO YOUNGER NEGRO ARTISTS

CHAPTER 1

African Exploration and Trade

1434-1800

Europe had so long been taught to regard the people who drink the waters of the Niger, the Gambia, and the Congo, who dwell on the borders of the Great Lakes and roam the plains of Nigeria as hopelessly degraded, that it came as a surprise—to not a few an agreeable surprise—to learn that these people had institutions worthy of study, of respect and of preservation.

Edward Wilmot Blyden, 1905
West Africa Before Europe

1434-1800

The first encounters between Europeans and the other—"other" most often referring to American Indians and Africans—is well documented through maps and travel accounts of European traders, explorers, and scientists. The earliest whites to visit the African continent were traders, although gold, trinkets, and other resources were not the only items exchanged. The interaction between Europeans and Africans transformed both continents in many ways, such as governing, culture, language, religion, foodways, dress, and ornamentation. Numerous considerably one-sided accounts by Europeans have survived and continue to be a major source for the study of early African cultures. Moorland's museum holdings are rich in African artifacts collected and donated by collectors and by visitors to various parts of the continent. Artifacts provide physical evidence of a historical tradition. Often viewed as objects of art, masks, figurines, and statues are functional and are used in religious and spiritual practices. In some cultures, items including combs, serving ware, and fabrics often denote status. Descriptions by Africans of their experiences are rare and valuable in that they provide a different perspective of first encounters with Europeans and their customs.

THE AFRICAN DIASPORA: REEXAMINING THE SOURCES

THE AFRICAN DIASPORA HAS THREE DIMENSIONS—the dispersion from Africa, settlement and adjustment abroad, and the physical and psychological return. The points of departure enable one to determine the general, if not the specific, area from which the Africans came; settlement and adjustment involve the establishment of residences and transforming encounters with the new human and material environment; and the return includes nostalgia for the homeland in its physical and psychological dimensions. The concept of diaspora thus extends the cultural continuity of dispersed people in the adopted homeland. We must remain mindful, however, that not all Africans who settled abroad were enslaved; many Africans traveled overseas as merchants, sailors, soldiers, entertainers, missionaries, adventurers, and so on.

Not only have diasporas influenced individual and local communities, they have had a major impact on national and international history and culture. It is interesting to speculate about the extent to which preconceived notions about dispersed people shaped their adjustments in foreign lands, as well as how memories of the original homeland have influenced social and cultural adjustments. In the case of Africans, preconceived myths and stereotypes have had a lasting effect on personal and group relationships. Yet too few studies have investigated in depth that aspect of Africa and its diaspora.

CEREMONIAL OBA MASK, Kingdom of Benin (Nigeria), 18th-19th century. Ivory. Sloan Collection.

From the times of classical writers and philosophers to contemporary times, Africans and their descendants have experienced personal and institutionalized racial and cultural stereotypes. Herodotus, for example, who is known as the father of history, wrote about Africans as savage animals and inferior beings. Solinus, a geographer of ancient times, characterized Africans as both "monstrous" and inferior. And the biblical interpretation of Noah's curse on Ham served as the framework that identified it with race and slavery. Jewish oral traditions also identified descendants of Ham as Black and slaves.

This history of stereotypes also included the Arab world. Historian Bernard Lewis and others have written about Arab and Persian inhabitants in the Middle East with strong feelings of contempt for Africans before and after the advent of Islam. Evidence shows that this characterization spread across much of Asia and continues, as does the idea in the Western world. More research is needed to flesh out all of the aspects of this phenomenon.

The point is that there existed a strong sense of African inferiority in Asia, the Middle East, Europe, and the Americas even before the development of the international trade in African slaves. Unfortunately, too few original sources of Africans and their descendants have been found; but it is also true that too few scholars have concentrated on Blacks in the ancient period. In some cases, there is the problem of identifying Africans who had Muslim names. However, Lewis and others have provided some clues. Note the "Crows of the Arabs," for example, who wrote in Arabic in the pre-Islamic era about the derogatory racial experiences they faced. Oral traditions in African history, music, and poetry also reveal some of the same issues. What is greatly required is a more thorough collection of these traditions, which may well be found in material collected by the United Nations Educational, Scientific and Cultural Organization and other organizations.

EXPLORERS AND MISSIONARIES IN PARTICULAR, among the first Asian and European visitors to Africa, have written about their experiences in the early stage of encounters with Africans. Although their focus was usually on trade and mission stations, they also commented on village life, customs, and government. Their comments normally included ethnocentric evaluations; therefore, a careful reading is required to deconstruct those accounts to show African creativity, political development, legal ideas, and an awareness of a wider world across their continent and the seas. Indeed, West Africans had notions about a world across the Atlantic before the exploration by Columbus. In fact, Columbus visited West Africa and consulted with local sailors before he ventured to the Americas. The evidence is very clear that North and East Africans sailed to areas along the Mediterranean, Red Sea, and Indian Ocean coasts. Again, references to these issues are frequently buried in sailors' accounts of other stories. A careful search with an eye for these examples very likely would be productive.

We know that slave ship captains kept records about enslaved Africans as commodities, but much more is known today about them as human beings. African place and ethnic names are recorded in ship logs, bills of sale, etc. Accounts of slave mutinies can be helpful in identifying African initiatives to rebel. What Africans ate on board ship, their physical routine, and the opportunities for interaction with their enslaved shipmates can be gleaned from ship records and the accounts of ship captains.

How many examples can be found of training in preparation for travel to Africa by explorers? Prince Henry the Navigator is perhaps the best example to date, but there very likely were others that had available to them written accounts of African villages, traders, and sailors. To what extent did these accounts and general perceptions of Africans affect that initial encounter with Africans on the continent? We also know that Europeans trained a number of Africans as translators and guides, but that such enterprises often turned into a trade in Africans. We need to know more about this aspect of the history of trade and exploration. A number of oral history projects have been conducted in Africa and should be examined for clues about the slave trade. Increasingly, African scholars are researching the slave trade in their own countries. Solid accounts about this have been written in Ghana, Benin, and Nigeria.

SIMILAR RESEARCH PROJECTS NEED TO BE DEVELOPED more aggressively in the diaspora, comprising the United States, the Caribbean, and South and Central America. Also, since most African students in the United States up to the 1960s attended historically Black colleges and universities, the accounts that they wrote about their own cultures and ancestral homelands for seminar papers, master's theses, and Ph.D. dissertations should prove to be valuable. In addition, a number of repositories maintain rare collections of books, pamphlets, and newspapers, some of which were written by Africans and other contemporary observers of exploration, the slave trade, and enslavement and their effects. Anthropologists Margaret Washington Creel and Sheila Walker have shown that religious and spiritual practices reveal African influences and the transformative process in parts of the Americas. Additional works along such lines have appeared in Spanish, Portuguese, and other languages.

Years ago, Howard University's Mark Hanna Watkins, a professor of anthropology, recorded and examined African languages with students in his class. Perhaps, he thought, those materials could help determine what the African students discussed in their own languages. The Moorland-Spingarn Research Center is favorably situated in an environment to locate, catalog, translate, and make available to others a significant body of these various data for research. Howard University's South African Research and Archival Project (SARAP), which identifies, inventories, and facilitates access to archival collections that show the connection between Americans and South Africans, has uncovered a considerable amount of documentation about early and contemporary African Americans. Several of the individuals identified in the 20th century had recollections about traditional and modern African societies and the encounters with foreigners, including African Americans.

These and other materials represent valuable sources whose full meaning has not yet been discovered, promising even more information, clarification, and understanding about the history of the African diaspora. —*Joseph Harris, professor emeritus, Howard University*

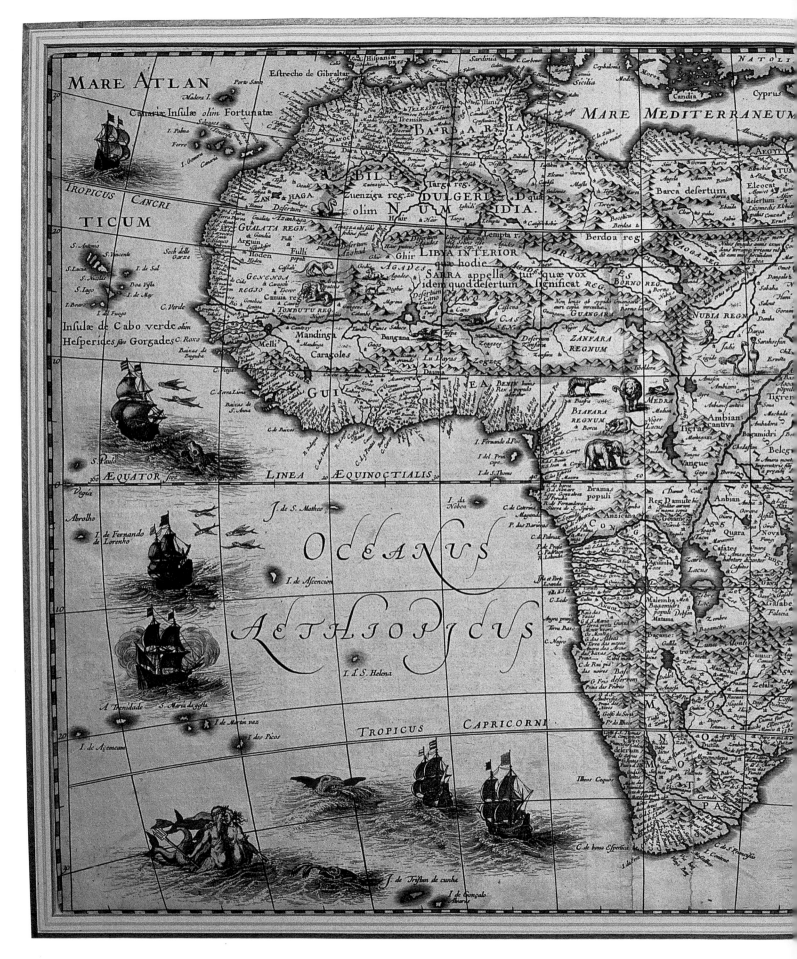

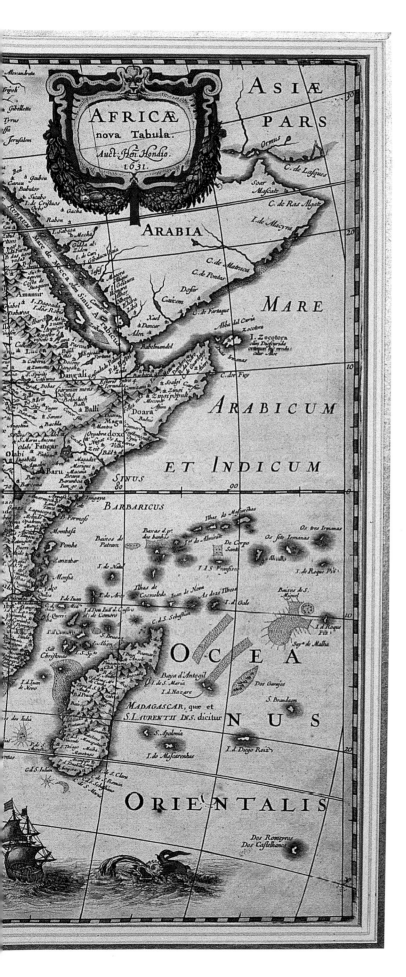

MAPPING AFRICA. During early maritime explorations of Africa in search of resources, Portuguese seamen defined Africa's coastline through cartography. The original intent was to find a shorter route to Asia by sailing around the southern coast of Africa. These early rare maps illustrate a lack of knowledge about Africa's interior; therefore, the geography beyond the detailed coastline is vague and sometimes inaccurate. The illustrations surrounding the continent represent superstitions that the uncharted waters around Africa held many unknown dangers, like sea monsters and serpents. Moorland's collection of maps covers the era of exploration through the present day.

"AFRICA NOVA TABULA," map by Henricus Hondius, Amsterdam, 1631. Hand-colored engraving. Cartographic Collection.

WEST AFRICA. The term West Africa loosely denotes the group of countries south of the Sahara and north of the Gulf of Guinea. It includes Nigeria, Ghana, Mali, and the Ivory Coast. This area appears in the earliest Arab records, particularly in descriptions of large, powerful cities of scholarship and trade, such as Tombouctou and Gao in Mali. These ancient civilizations were known for their centers of learning, which attracted students from all around.

West Africa is also noted for the early use of the lost-wax technique in casting brass, bronze, and gold. In this casting process, a wax model is coated with clay and then heated so that the wax melts, leaving a hollow mold into which metal can be poured. The technique may have been in practice in West Africa as early as A.D. 200, perfected by brass workers who were retained by royalty and the nobility.

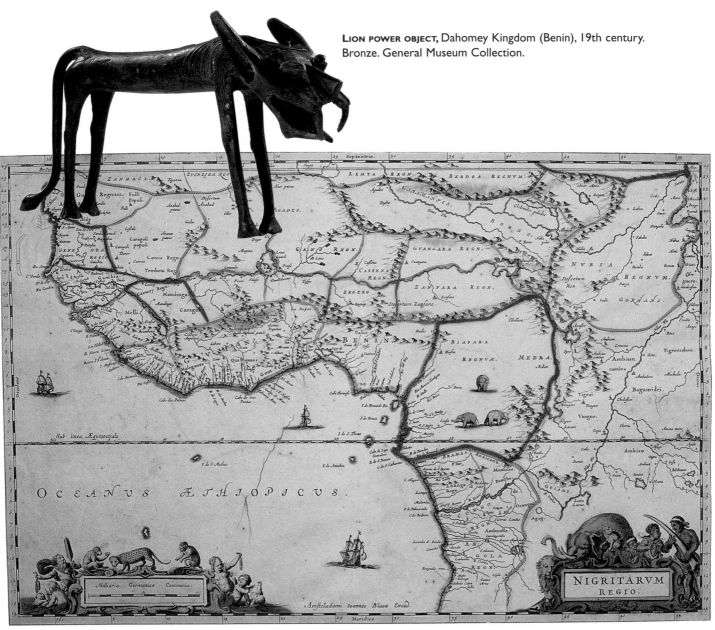

LION POWER OBJECT, Dahomey Kingdom (Benin), 19th century. Bronze. General Museum Collection.

"NIGRITARUM REGIO," map by Johannes Blaeu, Amsterdam, 1670. Hand-colored engraving. Cartographic Collection.

(OPPOSITE) **IFE (NIGERIA) HEAD,** 18th-19th century. Brass. General Museum Collection.

EAST AFRICAN CULTURES. Ethiopians can trace their nation's history back to antiquity. Located in the northeastern part of the continent, Ethiopia today has a culture that reveals the continuity of its long history. Proof of its past can be found on monuments and inscriptions. The country embraced Christianity as early as the second half of the fourth century, although Islamic influences can be found as well. Images of St. George, the patron saint of Ethiopia, grace triptychs, scrolls, and a variety of other media.

The Franklin H. Williams Collection specializes in artifacts that are used in religious ceremonies and social functions, whereas the museum's general collections include individual items of beauty and interest.

COPTIC HAND CROSSES CARRIED DURING SERVICES, 18th-19th century. Silver alloy and brass. Franklin H. Williams Collection.

BEGENNA (CEREMONIAL HARP), 19th-20th century. The begenna has eight to ten strings and is played only by men. Goatskin stretched on carved wooden frame. General Museum Collection.

(OPPOSITE) **"ST. GEORGE AND THE DRAGON,"** n.d. Tempura and ink on goatskin. General Museum Collection.

CENTRAL AND SOUTHERN AFRICA. In the early years of Portuguese exploration of West Africa, fears of mythical sea monsters and boiling equatorial waters discouraged exploration, but they also hint at early European travel down the coast to southern Africa.

Central and southern Africa were explored by Europeans after trade was well established with West African nations, and it was not until 1487 that navigators first rounded the Cape of Good Hope. Central African countries, including Gabon, Zaire, and the Congo, came to be known for their metalwork. The southern Africa region, which includes present-day South Africa and Mozambique, is considered to be the cradle of mankind, and its history is well documented.

"PORTRAITS OF AFRICAN SLAVES," *Gleason's Pictorial Drawing Room Companion,* 1850s. Prints and Photographs.

BEADED WALKING STICK, possibly Zulu, 19th-20th century. Wood with stringed beads. Cane Collection.

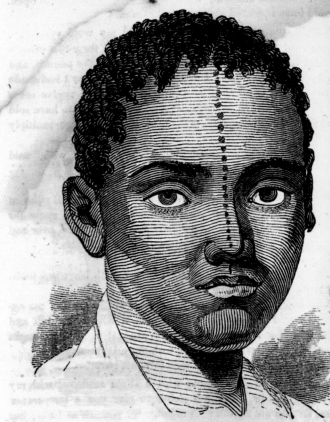

PORTRAITS OF AFRICAN SLAVES.

We present on the page herewith three characteristic port of Brazilian slaves. The marks discernible upon the faces of of the portraits are indelible, and caused by branding, a operation which these ignorant creatures voluntarily submi thinking these marks ornaments. Even Brazil has now jo with all the rest of the world in declaring the slave trade to piracy, and no more will be imported from Africa. Spain ostensibly done the same thing, but the authorities of Cuba at the business, and receive large bribes from the dealers in traffic. The portraits which we present are those of impo slaves, African born. Tattooing, or indelible marking of body, is very common in Africa, and indeed among very m other uncivilized races, people and countries, as the South

PORTRAIT OF A MOZAMBIQUE SLAVE WOMAN, IN BRA

Islanders, New Zealanders, etc., etc. The negro race of whic give the accompanying specimens, however, show a passion fo naments that amounts almost to a mania. The native regio the negro seems to be the central portion of Africa, though s tribes of the negro variety have been found in America and South Sea Islands. The negro formation prevails in Wes Africa in the region of the Gambia and Senegal; exten southwards, is most strongly marked in Guinea, and passes g ually over into the Caffre and Hottentot formation. Africa, it commences to the south of guebar and Monomote tribes known. ions, may have some e skin, but is by no means the only or the par cause of the black color, since, under the same climat the torrid zone, there are found all shades of complexion. W

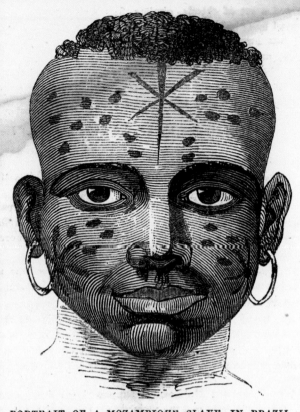

PORTRAIT OF A MOZAMBIQUE SLAVE, IN BRAZIL.

warmth of social affections. and a kindness and tenderness of feeling, which even the atrocities of foreign oppression have not been able to stifle. All travellers concur in describing the negro as mild, amiable, simple, hospitable, unsuspecting and faithful. They are passionately fond of music, and they express their hopes and fears in extemporary effusions of song. The opinion formerly maintained, that they were of an inferior variety of animals, would not now find an advocate, or a convert, even in the ignorance or the worst passions of the whites. Whether they are capable of reaching to the same height of intellectual cultivation as the Europeans, is a question on which we need more facts before any decision can be arrived at.

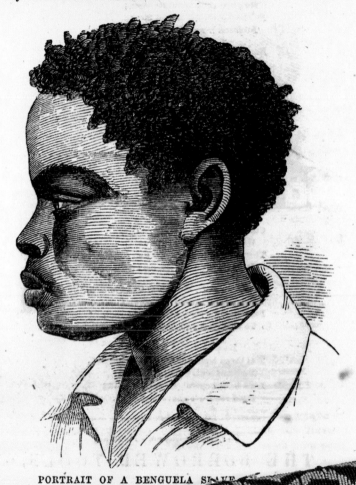

PORTRAIT OF A BENGUELA SLAVE

en in Africa only become somewhat swarthier, but never black, en in a succession of generations, unless they intermingle with e negroes; and blacks, in other regions and climates, are not and to lose their native hue. The seat of the black color is the e mucosum, and the external surface of the true skin, and en the *rete mucosum* is destroyed, as by disease, etc., the color lost; so, in parts of the body where the epidermis is unusually ck (the palms of the hand and the soles of the feet), it is of a hter shade. Negroes are also distinguished from the other es by other external, and by some anatomical peculiarities, rticularly in the conformation of the cranium. The projection the whole visage in advance of the forehead; the prolongation the upper and lower jaws; the small facial angle they evince, flatness of the forehead and of the hinder part of the head, gether with the compression in the direction of the temples, alving less space for the brain than in some other varieties; the olly, frizzled hair; the short, broad and flat nose; the thick, jecting lips, with many other peculiarities of formation, contute some of the characteristics of the negro or Ethiopic race. e African tribes of this variety have in general elevated th ves so far above the simple state of nature lower animals to subjection ctised a

ey have made simple despotisms, without ization. Their religion is merely the instinctive ression of the religious feeling in its lowest form of fetichism. eir languages are described as extremely rude and imperfect; ost destitute of construction, and incapable of expressing abactions. They have no art of conveying thoughts or events by ting, not even by the simplest symbolical characters. The ro character, if inferior in intellectual vigor, is marked by a

ferocious animal. argest and most powerful of the uger is found only in the East Indies, in Hindoostan, Siam, Cochin-China, Malacca and the isles of Sunda. Its strength and sanguinary disposition are such that it is the terror of the inhabitants in those countries; and no animal, except the elephant, is capable of resisting it. It even comes into the midst of villages, in the night time, for the purpose of carrying off cattle. The color is yellow, with transverse black stripes; and the tail has alternate black and yellow rings. The pupil of the eye is round. It resembles the other animals of the cat tribe in every respect, and can be tamed as easily as the lion. Its voice is very powerful, and resembles that of the lion.

THE IMAGE OF AFRICA IN THE AGE OF EXPLORATION

DURING THE AGE OF EXPLORATION, Africans did not designate themselves as Black, or even as Africans, but as members of their own myriad cultures. Defining sub-Saharan Africans as Black was part of Europeans' process of defining themselves at that time. At first, there were a number of competing images of Africans, but eventually those images crystallized into a small set of overly simplified, negative stereotypes widely shared in the West, and to some extent around the world.

Early on, Africans were felt by people in the Americas to hold a status relatively equal to that of Europeans. By the end of the 18th century, though, images of the African as inferior were being used to justify the slave trade. Modern capitalism found it profitable to employ stereotypes of Blacks as exotic or erotic, backed up by claims of science.

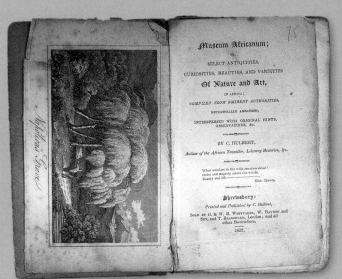

Further complicating the characterization of Africans was the broad spectrum of definitions concerning Black identity. Only in the U.S.—and only after the age of exploration— was it defined as anyone with African ancestry. European societies elsewhere in the Americas, Africa, and the rest of the world placed more significance on varying shades of color, resorting to such terms as "mulatto," "black," "Ethiopian," "African," "*moro*," "*nero*," "negro," "*negre*," "*preto*," and "*indiani*." In Brazil, dozens of terms evolved to describe degrees of color and related social status.

Powerful stereotypes emerged by the end of the 16th century, caricaturing the Black slave as happy-go-lucky, lazy, and irresponsible and overshadowing others that might have allowed for a more balanced picture. For example, Africans participated in European exploration: as interpreters in Africa; among Columbus's crews; and in the early conquests of Mexico and South America. There were many Black servants, slaves, and even executioners in Europe and its empires, but there were also many free Blacks among the populace, working as musicians, soldiers, or sailors. The European elite sometimes included African nobles, government officials, intellectuals, priests, and even saints.

Paradoxes abound. Europeans may have invoked the mythic curse of Ham as a basis for enslaving Blacks, but that did not alter the veneration of Black madonnas in Europe and the Americas. And although travel literature and the graphic arts, including marginal decoration on maps, might reinforce stereotypes, other representations portrayed beautiful Africans. Folklore, music, poems, and plays sometimes carried negative images but at other times revered qualities thought of as African. History provided plenty of positive images, but socioeconomic and intellectual developments determined otherwise. —*Allison Blakely, Boston University*

MUSEUM AFRICANUM; OR, SELECT ANTIQUITIES, CURIOSITIES, BEAUTIES, AND VARIETIES OF NATURE AND ART IN AFRICA, by Charles Hulbert, London, 1822. Library Collection.

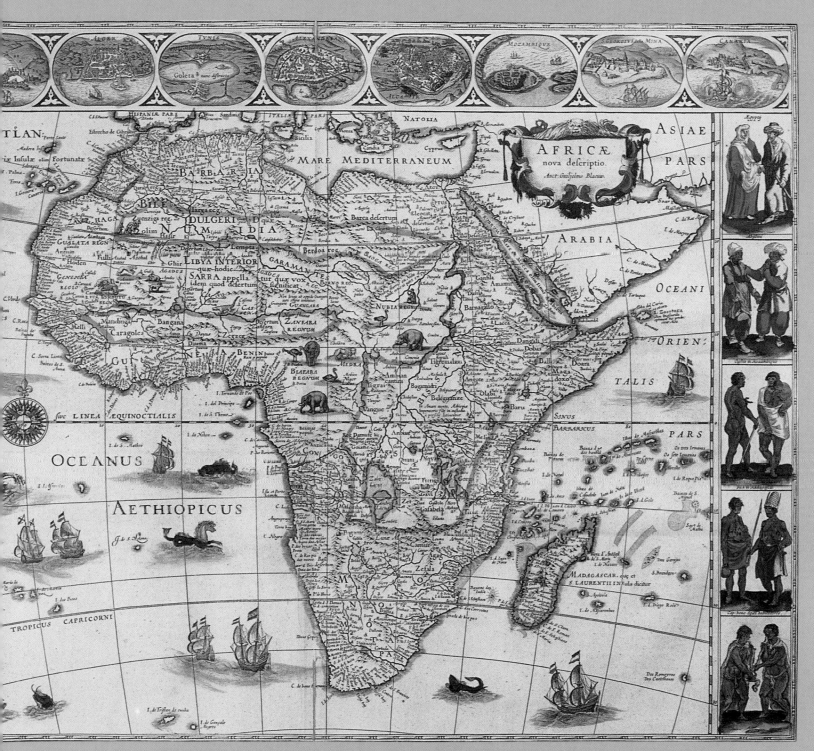

"AFRICA NOVA DESCRIPTIO," map by Willem Jansz Blaeu, Amsterdam, 1630. Hand-colored engraving. Cartographic Collection.

MONSIEUR DE St. GEORGE.

From an Original Picture in Mr. H. Angelo's Academy

AFRICANS IN EUROPE. Even before the commencement of the transatlantic slave trade, cultural exchanges between Europeans and Africans had already begun. These encounters heightened ideas about differences in color, intelligence, class, and civility, further defining racial identities and cementing concepts of inferiority.

Very little record exists of African experiences with the early Portuguese traders. Personal accounts of Africans living in Europe and written descriptions by captured Africans of their experiences provide some insight into the lives of Africans at this time, but life experiences vary widely.

Juan Latino—considered the first person of sub-Saharan African descent to publish a book of poems in a Western language (Latin)—was born in 1518. He later taught Latin grammar in Granada, Spain. Le Chevalier de Saint-George—a Black classical violinist and composer who studied music in Paris—was born in the West Indies in 1739, his father a French nobleman and plantation owner, his mother a Black slave from Guadeloupe.

AD CATHOLICUM PARITER ET INVICTISSIMUM PHILIPPUM DEI GRATIA HISPANIARUM REGUM, by Juan Latino, Granada, Spain, 1573. Library Collection.

(OPPOSITE) **"MONSIEUR DE ST. GEORGE,"** portrait by William Ward after a painting by Mather Brown, London, 1788. Colored mezzotint. General Museum Collection.

CHAPTER 2
The Transatlantic Slave Trade
1450-1860s

No one who has never seen a slave-deck can form an idea of its horrors. Imagine a deck about 20 feet wide, and perhaps 120 feet long, and 5 feet high. Imagine this to be the place of abode and sleep, during long, hot breathless nights, of 720 human beings! At sundown, when they were carried below, trained slaves received the poor wretches one by one, and laying each creature on his side in the wings, packed the next against him, and the next, and the next, and so on, till, like so many spoons packed away, they fitted into each other, a living mass. Just as they were packed, so must they remain, for the pressure prevented any movement, or the turning of the hand or foot, until the next morning when from their terrible night of horror they were brought on deck once more, weak, and worn, and sick. Then, after all had come up and received the bath mentioned [a saltwater bath by the hose-pipe of the pumps], there was the invariable horror of bringing up the bodies of those who had died during the night. One by one, they were cast overboard— a splash the only ceremony.

The Interesting Narrative of the Life of Olaudah Equiano, or Gustavus Vassa, the African, 1794

"I LEANED OVER THE MAIN HATCHWAY HOLDING A LANTERN."

1450-1860s   *Between the 15th and 19th centuries, European expansion into Africa stimulated drastic cultural, political, and economic change on both continents. What began as trade in goods evolved into trafficking in human beings. Between the early 1400s and the mid-19th century, an estimated 12 million to 20 million Africans were uprooted from their homeland and enslaved for labor in Europe, the Caribbean, the Americas, and other parts of the world. Traffickers captured Africans mostly from central Africa and from countries along the west coast, sometimes with the assistance of tribal leaders. Others fought the European invasion. Queen Nzinga (1583-1663) lived and ruled in regions south of the Congo River. She led numerous battles against the Portuguese in their efforts to invade central Africa, seeking slaves. Written accounts of Africans who survived transportation across the ocean into slavery describe in great detail the trek from inland Africa to the coast and the voyage across the ocean. They are often graphic in relaying the process of being stripped of one's native culture. The cruelty to which these Africans were subjected during the Middle Passage is unimaginable, and their eyewitness accounts added fuel to efforts to end slavery in later years.*

THE TRANSATLANTIC SLAVE SYSTEM

MIGRATION IS THE CENTRAL ELEMENT in world history. Initial human migration throughout and out of Africa preceded and enabled all others, and its engine was the forced relocation and chattel enslavement of African people from the 15th century through the 19th. That trauma nurtured the constellation of modern European nation-states built with unprecedented material wealth generated by conscripted African labor, and a global transformation emerged. The beginning of this process has been collapsed and inscribed vaguely in the popular world imagination in a single phrase: the transatlantic slave trade. It remains the largest and longest ongoing crime against humanity in modern world history, with the victims' economic, social, and cultural life force mingled inextricably in the veins of five continents, scores of national histories, and countless fragments of memory and meaning.

Trafficking in African humanity involved several stages: inland abduction, overland trek, and coastal imprisonment; the transatlantic oceanic ordeal (the Middle Passage); and the eventual struggle to form community and resist subjugation upon survival, arrival, and mixture with thousands of others from around and across the African continent. War prisoners and refugees, victims of raids and kidnappings, and criminal convicts provided the human capital supplied by African middlemen to meet the seemingly insatiable demand of the Dutch, Portuguese, Spanish, French, and English. Africans could be forced to walk from 60 to 400 miles to the coast, at a loss of life of from 10 percent

SLAVES IN THE HOLD OF A SLAVE SHIP, from "Capture of the Slave-ship 'Cora,'" *Century Illustrated Monthly Magazine,* vol. 48, no. 11, May 1, 1894. Omnium Gatherum Collection.

to up to 40 percent. Africans were sold to Europeans in small groups at makeshift prisons along the coast. Many scholars estimate that there were approximately 50 million people in Africa in 1700, half of whom were exposed to the trade in enslaved Africans. Fewer than two of every three abducted Africans ever reached the coast, scholars hypothesize, thus allowing sophisticated estimates of the total number of African lives lost in the process.

COASTAL PRISONS CALLED BARRACOONS ranged from outdoor fenced pens, to enclosed areas connected to a complex of warehouses, to full-fledged forts—more properly dungeons—where Europeans and Afro-Europeans lived while managing the trade. Some Africans were actually taken to small boats offshore to await deportation. Rape, murder, starvation, and conscript labor marked the often months-long African stays there. Africans were baptized and frequently branded by searing cross-shaped irons, marking the so-called conversion to Christianity, which became a rationale for both their enslavement and—when that was no longer economically feasible—their emancipation.

Vessels ranging from small sloops and schooners to three-masted ships of three decks anchored several miles offshore, and Africans were loaded onto them from canoes. They were moved onto the ships in groups of less than five, up to ten per day, so that it could take anywhere from two to six months to fill a port-hopping ship. Most vessels made few voyages and transported between 250 and 300 Africans. In a final humiliation, Africans were stripped of all clothing.

Between 5 percent and 20 percent of Africans (and 15 percent to 20 percent of the ships' crews) died during the several months of the crossing, from physical violence in the face of resistance, dehydration, smallpox, measles, gastrointestinal diseases, resistance to eating, and jumping overboard, among other reasons. Whites held physical power over Blacks, forming the basis both for African skepticism toward European institutions and racial solidarity. Sexual violence toward African women proved another bonding catalyst. People of different nations began to see themselves as African, sharing an identity, as they struggled to survive and resist their common oppressors and oppression.

Upon disembarking, Africans were packaged for sale on ship decks, in holding pens, or at sale houses. They then undertook what has been called the seasoning period, during which Africans adjusted to brutal physical enslavement, new languages, food, families, and worldviews. Between one-quarter and one-third of Africans who survived the Middle Passage did not survive this period, which could last up to three years. Ultimately, according to historian of slavery Joseph Miller, fewer than four out of every ten Africans initially abducted from their homes survived to start life in the Americas.

Africans found themselves working the sugar, tobacco, gold, and diamond fields of Brazil (the destination of nearly 40 percent of all abducted Africans); the gold and silver mines of Spanish South America and Mesoamerica; the sugarcane, coffee, cocoa, and livestock plantations of the Spanish, British, and French Caribbean islands; and tobacco, rice, sugar, and indigo fields in British North America. Cotton became king in 19th-century United States, and by 1860 Africans born in domestic enslavement—their owners would say "bred" to pick it—could cost up to the equivalent of $30,000 today. Africans were worth more at that time than all the physical property in the country and all the money in U.S. banks. The control over who would benefit from the material resources generated by the labor of the enslaved was the primary reason for the Civil War in the United States.

Estimates by historian Philip Curtain contend that it is possible that Africa experienced a decrease from 0.5 percent to less than 0.2 percent annual population growth over the course of deportation, in spite of the introduction of non-African foodstuffs, such as maize, which spurred population growth. Not only were Africans lost by abduction, death, or deportation, but the potential for population growth and even replenishment decreased due to the abduction. Some estimate that as many as 14 million possible births did not take place in Africa because potential parents were taken, an impact that significantly affected the population growth rate on the continent.

Enslavement ended throughout the hemisphere when it became economically unfeasible, politically insufferable, and legally unenforceable. European slave-trading nations abolished the international trade between 1802 and 1818. Britain outlawed the institution outright in 1838 and sent its ships into the Atlantic to enforce the ban. African resistance (and, in the case of the U.S. Civil War, withholding of plantation labor) was the perpetual pressure that ultimately realized emancipation, from Haiti (1793), to Jamaica (1834), to the U.S. (1865), Cuba (1886), and Brazil (1888), among others.

A GLOBAL POPULATION EXPLOSION and migration drew lower classes of Europeans to the Western Hemisphere, where they scratched out work in the system set in motion by African labor. Pulled across the Atlantic in several waves to work in systems of indenture and low-wage exploitation, they eventually replaced chattel enslavement. Those lower-class immigrants also received the unexpected benefit of access to "whiteness," a status to be earned by deliberately distancing from each country's population of Africans. African descendants remained legally, economically, politically, and culturally circumscribed reservoirs of "anti-citizens," and their status also perpetuated each country's illusion of the European roots of its perceived cultural superiority. This multinational European labor force was absorbed into the structure of each modern European nation-state on both sides of the Atlantic, leading to the ongoing experiments in 18th-, 19th-, and 20th-century Western-style capitalism and democracy. These states also exerted increasing control over land, people, and resources in the second stage of the age of Europe, known as colonialism in Africa, Latin America, Asia, and the Middle East.

Contests over control of these resources, contests of control by one nation over another, and contests over new non-European populations with desired resources led to the major world conflicts of the 19th and 20th centuries and previewed major conflicts with other international actors—Saudi Arabia, China, and India, for example—of the 21st century. As a tool to advocate for global African interests amid these global contests, the descendants of enslaved Africans created pan-Africanism, a movement that seeks to create a global African community.

Finally, the resources and economies of the former European colonies—and the economic position of Africans still trapped by their institutional disadvantages and cultural prejudices, suffering under the same logic of race that justified their ancestors' capture and exploitation—remain tied to the arrangement begun under the transatlantic trade system. —*Greg E. Carr, Howard University*

THE AFRICANS OF THE SLAVE BARK "WILDFIRE."—[From our own Correspondent.]

THE SLAVE DECK OF THE BARK "WILDFIRE," BROUGHT INTO KEY WEST ON APRIL 30, 1860.—[From a Daguerreotype.]

KEY WEST, FLORIDA, May 20, 1860.

ON the morning of the 30th of April last, the United States steamer *Mohawk*, Lieutenant Craven commanding, came to anchor in the harbor of this place, having in tow a bark of the burden of about three hundred and thirty tons, supposed to be the bark *Wildfire*, lately owned in the city of New York. The bark had on board five hundred and ten native Africans, taken on board in the River Congo, on the west side of the continent of Africa. She had been captured a few days previously by Lieutenant Craven within sight of the northern coast of Cuba, as an American vessel employed in violating our laws against the slave-trade. She had left the Congo River thirty-six days before her capture.

Soon after the bark was anchored we repaired on board, and on passing over the side saw, on the deck of the vessel, about four hundred and fifty native Africans, in a state of entire nudity, in a sitting or squatting posture, the most of them having their knees elevated so as to form a resting-place for their heads and arms. They sat very close together, mostly on either side of the vessel, forward and aft, leaving a narrow open space along the line of the centre for the crew of the vessel to pass to and fro. About fifty of them were full-grown young men, and about four hundred were boys aged from ten to sixteen years. It is said by persons acquainted with the slave-trade and who saw them, that they were generally in a very good condition of health and flesh, as compared with other similar cargoes, owing to the fact that they had not been so much crowded together on board as is common in slave voyages, and had been better fed than usual. It is said that the bark is capable of carrying, and was prepared to carry, one thousand, but not being able without inconvenient delay to procure so many, she sailed with six hundred. Ninety and upward had died on the voyage. But this is considered as comparatively a small loss, showing that they had been better cared for than usual. Ten more have died since their arrival, and there are about forty more sick in the hospital. We saw

on board about six or seven boys and men greatly emaciated, and diseased past recovery, and about a hundred that showed decided evidences of suffering from inanition, exhaustion, and disease. Dysentery was the principal disease. But notwithstanding their sufferings, we could not be otherwise than interested and amused at their strange looks, motions, and actions. The well ones looked happy and contented, and were ready at any moment to join in a song or a dance whenever they were directed to do so by "Jack"—a little fellow as black as ebony, about twelve years old, having a handsome and expressive face, an intelligent look, and a sparkling eye. The sailors on the voyage had dressed "Jack" in sailor costume, and had made him a great pet. When we were on board "Jack" carried about in his hand a short cord, not only as the emblem but also as the instrument of his brief delegated authority. He would make the men and boys stand up, sit down, sing, or dance just as he directed. When they sang "Jack" moved around among them as light as a cat, and beat the time by

slapping his hands together, and if any refused to sing, or sang out of time, Jack's cord descended on their backs. Their singing was monotonous. The words we did not understand. We have rarely seen a more happy and merry-looking fellow than "Jack."

From the deck we descended into the cabin, where we saw sixty or seventy women and young girls, in Nature's dress, some sitting on the floor and others on the lockers, and some sick ones lying in the berths. Four or five of them were a good deal tattooed on the back and arms, and we noticed that three had an arm branded with the figure "7," which, we suppose, is the merchant's mark.

On the day of their arrival the sickest, about forty in all, were landed and carried to a building on the public grounds belonging to Fort Taylor, and Doctors Whitehurst and Skrine employed as medical attendants. We visited them in the afternoon. The United States Marshal had procured for all of them shirts, and pants for the men, and some benevolent ladies of the city had sent the

MIDDLE PASSAGE. The Middle Passage is the name given to the transportation of slaves from the West African coast across the Atlantic to the Americas. The beginning passage was the trek of captured Africans from the inside of the continent to the coast for transport out; the final passage took them from landing in the New World to their destinations as slaves. It is estimated that between 12 million and 20 million Africans sailed the Middle Passage. Slave ships were crowded and unsanitary. As a result, disease spread quickly, and slave mortality was high. The first ships were merchant vessels, their holds altered with platforms to carry human cargo. As countries began to ban slave trafficking, faster ships such as the *Ouragan* were built to outrun slower capture vessels, and illegal trafficking continued. Following the capture of slavers like the *Wildfire*, intercepted en route to Cuba in 1860, the United States sought to return Blacks to Liberia on captured slave ships.

(*OPPOSITE*) **"THE SLAVE DECK OF THE BARK 'WILDFIRE,' "** *Harper's Weekly,* June 2, 1860. Illustrated Newspaper Collection.

(*RIGHT*) **REPLICA OF THE *OURAGAN*,** a converted slave ship known for its speed. Ambassador Ronald D. Palmer Papers.

(*BELOW*) **"THE SLAVE SHIP—SIGHTING AN ENGLISH CRUISER,"** *Harper's Weekly,* April 25, 1874. Illustrated Newspaper Collection.

THE SLAVE-SHIP—SIGHTING AN ENGLISH CRUISER.

BECOMING AFRICAN AMERICAN

HISTORIANS ESTIMATE that of the approximately 11 million captured Africans who survived the voyage across the Atlantic Ocean, about 4 percent, or almost half a million, were brought to colonial North America before the slave trade was made illegal in 1808. New arrivals came from varying African countries and cultural groups with distinct differences in language and customs and interacted with enslaved persons who were born on American soil. To control the captives and prevent revolts, Africans were routinely separated from family and friends. Those who spoke the same language or shared the same culture were divided as well. They had to find their own means

of communicating with each other, often relying upon elements from their native culture and incorporating them into American customs. As a result, persons from diverse African societies formed new friendships, started new families, and created a new culture.

Forced to learn the English language and culture, and also to accept Christianity, Africans were unable to maintain the language and customs of any specific ethnic group in Africa, but they did not forget or abandon the values and practices they absorbed in their home societies. Historians before the 1960s believed that almost all traces of African cultures vanished during the experience of slavery, but contemporary research of plantation culture has uncovered evidence of African roots in dance, music, foodways, religion, language, and folktales.

A different interpretation emerged in the 1970s, therefore. At that time, John Blassingame, Herbert Gutman, and other scholars detailed the survival of African values and cultural practices as materials that formed the basis of a new African-American culture that developed as new families and communities were created.

Africans used the customs and values they had in common to create a new culture that was a fusion of African and European traditions. Placing a high value upon the extended family, Africans treated other slaves as extended kin, regardless of blood ties. In the 1600s and 1700s, Africans developed a significant degree of cultural independence from white slave owners. The marriage rules, naming patterns, speech and language patterns, and social customs practiced by Africans were often the opposite of those practiced by white Americans.

The new families, new kin relations, new values, and new customs became the foundation of a newly African-based family life and identity—the beginning of what we now know as African-American culture. —De Witt S. Dykes, Jr., Oakland University

ENGRAVING OF WOMAN BEING BEATEN ABOARD SLAVE SHIP, from *The Iniquity of the Slave Trade! An Account of the Murder of a Female Negro, who Was Flogged to Death by Order of an Unmerciful Captain…* Religious Tract Society, London, ca 1820. Library Collection.

4ᵉ.Div.

Dess d'apr nat par Re...

Pl. 1.

Lith de Engelmann, rue du Fault Montmartre N° 6, à Paris.

Deroi del.

NÈGRES A FOND DE CALLE.

"NÈGRES A FOND DE CALLE," artist unknown, 1835. Lithograph. Prints and Photographs.

London Sepr. 30th, 1794 —

My very Dr & Worthy friends &c.

This with my best respect to you & family hope you are all well as I am & mine with many thanks to our almighty God for his every favours — Dr Sir not having any of my narrative Left to take to any of the places that you were please to give me recommendations to — I came here on the 11th. Inst. & have finished on Saturday Last another small Edition Viz. 500 Copies of my Life — with which I mean next week to go to Bocking & Manningtree Thro, Chelmsford — & visit Bury & then to Lynn & Wisbech — & afterwards use your very kind Letters — This Edition is 5. a Copy, & has some additions — printed on 20 = ream paper which is about the Quality of the paper that you have — I hope you got the

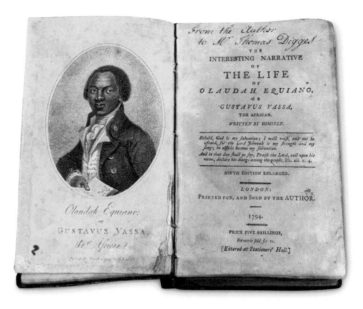

THE INTERESTING NARRATIVE OF THE LIFE OF OLAUDAH EQUIANO, OR GUSTAVUS VASSA, THE AFRICAN. WRITTEN BY HIMSELF, London, 1794. Ninth edition book with inscription to Thomas Diggs. Library Collection.

(LEFT AND BELOW) **CORRESPONDENCE (FRONT AND BACK) FROM OLAUDAH EQUIANO TO THOMAS DIGGS.** September 30, 1794. General Museum Collection.

the Letter ~~I sent~~ I sent to you in may. if So. I am Sorry in not hearing from you. I beg you will be kind enough to make my best respect to Mr & Mrs Printice & the friendly Revd. Mr read. & all others of my Worthy acquantences —

Dr Sir if you think it Convenient. I will be very much obliged to you for few Lines to the good Lady that you were please to mention to me — about newington — or Else where —

I hope one time or another to have the Heart felt fatisfaction to see you again — I have indulged my self to insert your name in the List of the Subscribers — in my book out of great respect — & also the Revd Dr Temple Dr Friends. I am with Christian Love & Gratitude & many

many prayers. for your Soul, & bodily well fare — to that God who ever regards the prayers of faith — may he give you & yrs both the upper & the nether Spring Blessings — — Adieu &c. Gustavus Vassa The African

at Mr Hamiltons No 30 Eagle Street Holborn London

(OPPOSITE) **THE INTERESTING NARRATIVE OF THE LIFE OF OLAUDAH EQUIANO, OR GUSTAVUS VASSA, THE AFRICAN. WRITTEN BY HIMSELF,** Dublin, 1791. Fourth edition with inscription about his marriage in 1792. Library Collection.

NARRATIVE OF OLAUDAH EQUIANO. Olaudah Equiano (1745?-1797), sailor, author, and abolitionist, was born the son of a Nigerian tribal chief and captured as a child. He was taken to Virginia and sold to a lieutenant in the Royal Navy, than transported to England. His owner renamed him Gustavus Vassa after a 16th-century Swedish king. After working for his master on a ship for several years, Equiano requested his promised freedom. His master responded angrily, sending him to the West Indies to be sold. There he was purchased by a Philadelphia Quaker, who allowed him to buy his freedom in 1766. In the 1780s, Equiano decided to chronicle his experiences and observations of slavery. His book was first published in 1789. Eight editions were published in Great Britain and one in America during his lifetime. Moorland has at least one copy of each edition, including a 1794 edition signed by the author to his friend Thomas Diggs, and a fourth edition containing Equiano's notation of his marriage in 1792.

Weit von meinem Vaterlande
Muß ich hie verschmachten und vergehn,
Ohne Trost, in Müh' und Schande;
O, die weißen Männer! klug und schön!!

Der Neger
in
Westindien.

Und ich hab' den
Nichts gethan!
Die im Himmel,
Schwarzen Man

ohn Erbarmen
mir armen

Nürnberg bei Friedrich Campe.

INTO THE CARIBBEAN. By the end of the 18th century, Britain led the slave trade. Most slaves were being transported to the Caribbean and South America, where the West Indian colonies, including Jamaica and Barbados, were prized and profitable because of their sugar production. Life was brutal. Profits were valued far above life itself, or at least the lives of the slaves who worked the plantations. Slave narratives attest to the brutality of sugar plantation life in the West Indies and the cruelty suffered at the hands of planters. *"Der Neger in Westindien"* "(The Negro in the West Indies)," a lithograph published by Friedrich Campe (1777-1846), a German printer and publisher, clearly illustrates the human degradation of slavery. A manacled slave kneels, probably begging for mercy, in the shadow of the planter, who holds a whip at his side. Slaves work in sugarcane fields in the background.

"DER NEGER IN WESTINDIEN," by Friedrich Campe, Nuremberg, 18th century. Hand-colored lithograph. Prints and Photographs.

CHAPTER 3

The Experience of Enslavement

1619-1865

Let us look at the objects for which the Constitution was framed and adopted, and see if slavery is one of them. Here are its own objects as set forth by itself:—"We, the people of these United States, in order to form a more perfect union, establish justice, ensure domestic tranquility, provide for the common defense, promote the general welfare, and secure the blessings of liberty to ourselves and our posterity, do ordain and establish this Constitution of the United States of America." The objects here set forth are six in number: union, defence, welfare, tranquility, justice, and liberty. These are all good objects, and slavery, so far from being among them, it is a foe of them all.

Frederick Douglass, March 26, 1860
Speech, "The Constitution of the United States:
Is It Pro-Slavery or Anti-Slavery?"

A PRIME AND ORDERLY GANG OF

68 Long Cotton Field Negroes,

Belonging to the Estate of the late Christopher J. Whaley.

WILBUR & SON

Will sell at PUBLIC AUCTION in Charleston,

At the Mart in Chalmers Street,

On Thursday, Feb. 2d, 1860,

COMMENCING AT ELEVEN O'CLOCK,

THE FOLLOWING GANG OF LONG COTTON NEGROES,

Who are said to be remarkably prime, and will be sold as per Catalogue.

NAMES.		AGES.	NAMES.		AGES.
Jimmy,	driver,	30	Carter,		36
Flora,	seamstress,	24	Taffy,		13
James,		5	Rachel,	($ 720,)	8
Charles,	($ 125,)	1	Jannett,		18
August,		52	Phebe,	($ 860,)	40
Mathias,	($ 1,220,)	18	Judy,		8
Sandy,		16	Major,		40
John,		13	Lavinia,		30
Tom,		70	Billy,	($ 550,)	10
Jack,		38	Tamor,		6
James,		6	Jimmy,		52
Leah,		5	Kate,		46
Flora,		2	Susan,		25
Andrew,		42	Thomas,	($ 380,)	6
Binah,		40	Kate,		1
Phillis,		20	Edward,	coachman,	49
Mary,		15	Amey,		22
Lymus,		10	Teneh,	washer,	30
Abram,	($ 275,)	2	Josephine,		9
Binah,		2 mos.	Sam,		11
Andrew,		29	Isaac,		5
Hagar,		25	William,		1
Dayman,		4	Amey,		27
Cuffy,		21	Louisa,	($ 750,)	8
Hagar,	($ 1,320,)	20	Joe,		3
Margaret,		85	Sam,	ruptured,	65
Lucy,	cripple,	60	Andrew,	dropsical,	61
John,		22	Daniel,		70
Ellick,	($ 1,160,)	18	Lymus,		30
Libby,		19	Lucy,	nurse,	58

TERMS.

One-third Cash; balance in one and two years, secured by bond, and mortgage of the negroes, with approved personal security. Purchasers to pay us for papers.

1619-1865

In the first decades of American freedom, the country quickly became a political and economic world force. Yet even while Americans fought for their freedom from Britain, the Declaration of Independence did not extend to African Americans. Neither did the U.S. Constitution. The type of slavery practiced in America was chattel slavery, the legal ownership of one human being by another. The owner had a legal right to buy and sell at will, and like other property, slaves could be passed down from one generation to the next as inheritance. Chattel slaves were used for labor. What distinguished chattel slavery in America was the race factor. The enslavement of African people in America lasted 250 years. The word "slave" first appeared in 1656, in the records of colonial Virginia. At first, the laws were poorly defined, but as the demand for slaves grew, more laws were enacted that further defined and regulated slavery. "Slave for life" became standard text on bills of sale and in wills. The experience of enslavement, particularly the pain of separation from family and the treatment received at the hands of cruel masters, was related in autobiographies of former slaves including Venture Smith, Equiano, and Frederick Douglass.

SLAVERY AND THE AMERICAS

ENSLAVEMENT, BONDAGE, AND INVOLUNTARY SERVITUDE have existed for millennia as aspects of the human condition. Peoples of Africa enslaved each other, and were enslaved by others, for centuries before the coming of Europeans to Africa and the European discovery of the Americas. European exploration of the Americas in the late 15th century resulted in the wholesale removal of African populations from their homelands and their enslavement in the areas newly encountered. Although traditions among Native American peoples suggest an earlier arrival of Africans, their presence in the Americas is routinely seen as resulting from the European need to develop a stable labor force to help in the exploitation of the Americas and their newly discovered riches. All European nations involved in the exploration and colonization of the Americas were also active and willful participants in the enslavement of Africans and the destruction of both indigenous and African societies.

The depopulation and destruction of New World civilizations resulted through conquest by force of arms and the advent of diseases that decimated nonresistant populations. African societies suffered as a result of enslavement and the attendant depopulation of communities. This destruction began as early as 1493, when the explorer Christopher Columbus established the first permanent European colony at Hispaniola. In North America, the Spanish, Dutch, French, and English were all involved; the Portuguese were especially active in South America.

"68 LONG COTTON FIELD NEGROES," slave auction announcement, 1860. Broadside. Omnium Gatherum Collection.

Beginning with violent entrapment and capture, and continuing during the withering horror of the sea voyage known as the Middle Passage, rape, murder, violent assault, emotional and psychological destabilization, and forced labor often resulted in death. Such abuse of a commodity seemingly as valuable as a slave was tolerated due to the seemingly inexhaustible supply. African slaves became the fuel that fired the engines of capitalism. Paramount among its products were sugar and rum, cotton and tobacco. Among all other products, sugar had the earliest, longest, and greatest impact throughout the Americas in institutionalizing slavery and the plantation system from the late 15th century and early 16th century in Portuguese and Spanish America, until the late 19th century in Brazil.

What began in the 16th century as a barbaric trade in humans to exploit the world newly discovered by Europeans emerged at the dawning of the 21st century as a triumph of spirit, courage, and indomitable will over the forces of oppression and exploitation. While unknown numbers both perished in and successfully endured the horrors of the Middle Passage and the living hell that awaited, those that did carried the seeds of survival. Over the course of four centuries, their progeny would build the Americas and enrich Europe. They would die countless anonymous deaths and endure innumerable indignities and humiliations. But they would survive and their cultures would profoundly influence their new environments.

A DEFINING ASPECT OF THE EUROPEAN CONQUEST of the Americas is the extraordinary influence of African cultures in the New World. This is evident in language, music, foods and culinary arts, dance, artistic expressions, and a variety of talents that have been submerged within the larger context of creative arts and construction skills. Intellectual contributions were largely unrecognized, miscredited, or intentionally misappropriated. Everything about the conquest and domination of the Americas influenced Europe. The impact dominated politics and economics, as well as diplomatic and military relationships and antagonisms. The issue of slavery dominated the Americas and challenged religious concepts. Its ubiquity forever changed the relationships between Europe and Africa and between the fairer and darker-complected peoples of these opposing civilizations. This European domination would ultimately lead to a pseudoscientific and religious justification for the inferiority and enslavement of many millions of Africans—perhaps upwards of 20 million—and forever change the prospects of the African continent's viability for the benefit of its native populations. The rise of the Americas and the sustenance of Europe would be based upon the pillage of Africa and the murder, subjugation, and enslavement of its people from areas throughout the continent.

Although it is clear that people of African descent traveled with Spanish explorers to that part of North America that is today identified as the United States, their coming as enslaved people to Virginia in 1619 is traditionally identified as the beginning of slavery and the slave trade in the British colonies that would evolve some one and a half centuries later as the United States. The early diversity of slave communities in the New World reflected the wide range of European interest in both Africa and the Americas, built through the use of resources, both financial and material, to benefit the welfare of European society at the expense of Africans and the native peoples of the Americas and the

Caribbean. The extent of these European societies in the Americas varied, reflecting the vagaries of European geopolitics. Modern societies today reflect the early diverse and extended dominance of the Spanish, Portuguese, French, Dutch, and English.

Europeans destroyed native belief systems and replaced them with various forms of Catholic and Protestant Christianity. In many instances the new religion coexisted with other beliefs or was transformed by incorporating African and native beliefs. This is most evident with Candomblé in Brazil, Voudou in Haiti, Santería in Cuba, and other African-influenced beliefs elsewhere in the regions of enslavement. To the extent that customs and cultural practices were allowed to exist or to be displayed, those without obvious religious significance may have continued solely by virtue of the ignorance of European religious, political, and social authorities and the community at large. Christianity was to play a dominant role among the native and African peoples in the New World, many of whom widely adopted it, either through coercion or by their own free will. It is ironic that conquistadores and other explorers and despoilers justified their terrorism, destruction, murder, and enslavement as an extension of rights, even responsibilities, endorsed by most Christians and their church. Indeed, it was Ferdinand and Isabella of Spain who promoted their desires for conquest through Christopher Columbus and dehumanized native and African peoples. Rendering the natives and African savages beyond the protections of orthodox beliefs, they justified butchery and indiscriminate enslavement.

One of the greatest controls imposed upon enslaved African communities in the Caribbean was the essential isolation of these communities on islands. Refuge was found only in mountainous and forested areas, which offered sanctuary for escaped and liberated slaves. In Jamaica, Haiti, Barbados, and Cuba, Africans sought relief from chattel exploitation. African enslavement also extended to continental areas in Central and South America occupied by Europeans in their efforts to control the wealth and resources of the New World. Just as slave labor was necessary to exploit the agricultural opportunities of the more easily conquered, controlled, and dominated island territories, so too would slavery be a defining tool in the conquest and control of the continental mass. The remnants of French and Dutch influences in the New World reflect their primacy in Europe at various periods, while the extensive Portuguese presence in South America and the Spanish influence throughout the Americas reflect their early and long prominence in European exploration and geopolitical ascendancy. Although the Spanish, French, Dutch, and others all had a presence in continental North America, British influence would eventually dominate and supplant the strong Spanish and French presence. The New World experience is inevitably focused upon the British colonies in North America and the ascendance of the slavery-dominated society of the United States.

The history of the British colonies was marked by the ascendance of chattel slavery to support an economy based upon slave labor. The American war of independence from Britain was based upon ideals of freedom and democracy that were hypocritical in a social and economic system based upon slavery and human exploitation. This contradiction to the principle of freedom would haunt the nation and lead to a civil conflict that would define both the nation's past and future.
—*Thomas C. Battle, Howard University*

W. H. Brooke F.S.A.

SALE OF ESTATES, PICTURES AND SLAVES IN THE RO

THE SALE OF SLAVES. Enslaved Africans worked in the sugar plantations established in those parts of the Caribbean controlled by France and Great Britain, in the sugar plantations of South America, and in the tobacco plantations of colonial America. Slavery was slower to take hold in the colonies than in parts of the Americas farther south. But by the late 17th century, the slave trade grew and enslaved workers became more available and less expensive. Then American planters began to see some benefits in purchasing larger numbers of Africans to work the more profitable cotton plantations. Published slave narratives, deeds of sale, engravings, newspapers, and abolitionists' pamphlets from those times offer graphic details about the slavery experience, from the points of view of the owner and the slave, the entrepreneur and the abolitionist. These historic documents and contemporary ephemera can go far to dispel myths about slavery as an institution and as an experience. American slavery, for example, was not exclusively a southern practice, nor did slaves passively accept their fate.

(LEFT) **"SALE OF ESTATES, PICTURES AND SLAVES IN THE ROTUNDA, NEW ORLEANS,"** by W. H. Brooke and J. M. Starling, 1860. Engraving. Prints and Photographs.

DEED OF SALE, CAROLINE, "A SLAVE FOR LIFE," April 21, 1844 Omnium Gatherum Collection.

The State of Alabama } Before G W Benson
Autauga County } Judge of Probate of said County

The undersigned, one of the guardians of Louza
M Ziegler & Mary W Ziegler submits to your
honor the following report of the hire of the slaves
of said wards respectively for the year 1863.

The Slaves of L M Ziegler were hired as follows;

Henry, & wife & child to J J Dawson for		$ 103 00
Jane & child to P H D Bardelabun for		53 00
Adaline & 2 children to Jas Nunn for		19 00
Grad to I Nunn for		125 00
A small girl to W R Green "		10 00
Mary Jane to W B Jackson "		65 00
		$375.00

The Slaves of M W Ziegler were hired as follows;

Rody to E Golson for		75 00
Rachael " W B Jackson "		75 00
Martha " G W Smedly "		46 00
Jim " N G M Golson ,		110 00
		$306 00

Sworn to & subscribed before
me this 19th Oct 1863   N G M Golson

G W Benson

Judge

SLAVE WORK.

SLAVE WORK. The environments in which slaves carried out their labors varied tremendously, depending to some degree upon the location in which they worked. Northern states, without huge plantations, had no need for a mass labor force, so Northerners tended to purchase slaves as laborers, servants, and craftsmen. In the South, slaves performed the same duties in homes and workshops, but many others—the majority, in fact—worked in the fields from sunup to sundown, six days a week. They were given Sundays and Christmas Day off.

Africans who brought skills with them, such as ironwork or pottery, might find their work in settings outside their owners' homes. Slave owners hired out their skilled slaves to work in local foundries, in mills, on construction sites, and in other locations where they performed different services.

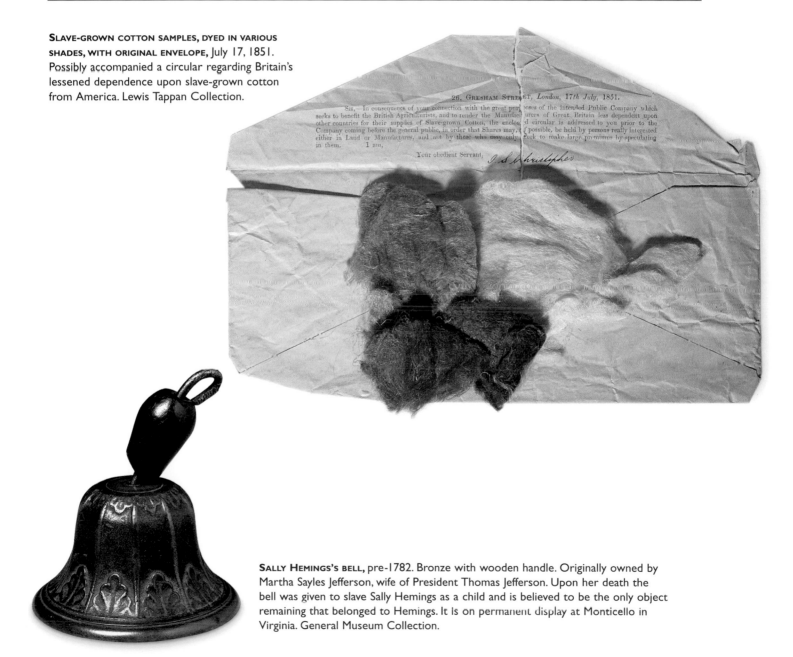

SLAVE-GROWN COTTON SAMPLES, DYED IN VARIOUS SHADES, WITH ORIGINAL ENVELOPE, July 17, 1851. Possibly accompanied a circular regarding Britain's lessened dependence upon slave-grown cotton from America. Lewis Tappan Collection.

SALLY HEMINGS'S BELL, pre-1782. Bronze with wooden handle. Originally owned by Martha Sayles Jefferson, wife of President Thomas Jefferson. Upon her death the bell was given to slave Sally Hemings as a child and is believed to be the only object remaining that belonged to Hemings. It is on permanent display at Monticello in Virginia. General Museum Collection.

(OPPOSITE) **LIST OF SLAVES HIRED OUT FROM L. M. ZEIGLER AND MARY W. ZEIGLER,** Alabama, 1863. Omnium Gatherum Collection.

RUNNING AWAY. The Fugitive Slave Act was part of a set of laws referred to as the Compromise of 1850, which helped ease the differences between advocates for and against slavery. It gave slaveholders the right to pursue fugitive slaves in any state and, in exchange, admitted California as a free state and prohibited slave trading in the District of Columbia. Abolitionists resented that the act gave rights to slaveholders, and in response activity increased along the Underground Railroad, the secretly planned passage from one safe haven to the next that escaping slaves could use to get north.

The desire for freedom caused many a slave to leave family and friends at the risk of capture, imprisonment, and severe punishment. Reward posters illustrate the lengths to which slaveholders were willing to go in order to have their runaways returned. Slave narratives and published accounts attest to the cruelty dealt to slaves who were indeed discovered, captured, and carried back to their owners.

Other historical evidence shows that freedom was not a one-way road. Although free Blacks carried papers proving their status as liberated citizens, some were kidnapped, carried back to the South, and sold back into slavery.

"SECRETS OF THE PRISON-HOUSE—A CELL IN THE FEMALE DEPARTMENT OF THE WASHINGTON JAIL.—FROM A SKETCH MADE ON THE SPOT BY OUR SPECIAL ARTIST, MR. LUMLEY.

"SECRETS OF THE PRISON-HOUSE—A CELL IN THE FEMALE DEPARTMENT OF THE WASHINGTON JAIL," *Frank Leslie's Illustrated Newspaper,* vol. 13, no. 318, December 28, 1861. Prints and Photographs.

(OPPOSITE) **RUNAWAY SLAVE REWARD POSTER,** St. Louis, Missouri, August 23, 1852. Omnium Gatherum Collection.

$2,500 REWARD!

RANAWAY, from the Subscriber, residing in Mississippi county, Mo., on Monday the 5th inst., my

Negro Man named GEORGE.

Said negro is five feet ten inches high, of dark complexion, he plays well on the Violin and several other instruments. He is a shrewd, smart fellow and of a very affable countenance, and is twenty-five years of age. If said negro is taken and confined in St. Louis Jail, or brought to this county so that I get him, the above reward of $1,000 will be promptly paid.

JOHN MEANS.

Also, from Radford E. Stanley,

A NEGRO MAN SLAVE, NAMED NOAH,

Full 6 feet high; black complexion; full eyes; free spoken and intelligent; will weigh about 180 pounds; 32 years old; had with him 2 or 3 suits of clothes, white hat, short blue blanket coat, a pair of saddle bags, a pocket compass, and supposed to have $350 or $400 with him.

ALSO---A NEGRO MAN NAMED HAMP,

Of dark copper color, big thick lips, about 6 feet high, weighs about 175 pounds, 36 years old, with a scar in the forehead from the kick of a horse; had a lump on one of his wrists and is left-handed. Had with him two suits of clothes, one a casinet or cloth coat and grey pants.

Also, Negro Man Slave named BOB,

Copper color, high cheek bones, 5 feet 11 inches high, weighs about 150 pounds, 22 years old, very white teeth and a space between the centre of the upper teeth Had a blue blanket sack coat with red striped linsey lining. Supposed to have two suits of clothes with him; is a little lame in one ancle.

$1,000 will be given for George----$600 for Noah---$450 for Hamp---$450 for Bob; if caught in a free State, or a reasonable compensation if caught in a Slave State, if delivered to the Subscribers in Miss. Co., Mo., or confined in Jail in St. Lonis, so that we get them Refer to

**JOHN MEANS &
R. E. STANLEY.**

ST. LOUIS, August 23, 1852. (PLEASE STICK UP.)

ENSLAVED CHILDREN IN THE UNITED STATES

OF THE AFRICANS TRANSPORTED from their places of birth and into the Americas, where they were indentured or enslaved, an estimated one-fourth to one-third were girls and boys. "If you have good trade, purchase forty or fifty Negroes," wrote slave trader William Ellery to the captain of his ship in 1746. "Get most of them mere Boys and Girls, some Men, let them be Young, No very small Children." On occasion, children made up the majority of a cargo. For example, the *Margarita* sailed in 1734 with 93 Africans aboard, 87 percent of whom were 16 or younger, making the average age about 13.

Most of the published narratives by young Middle Passage survivors recall an idyllic childhood.

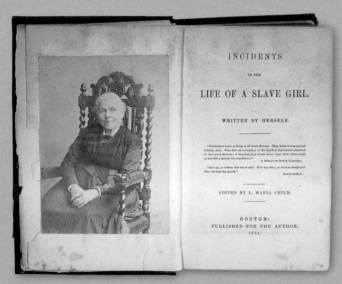

Florence Hall remembered playing in an open field when raiders grabbed her and her playmates. Ottobah Cugoano wrote about playing with 18 or 20 children when "snatched away." The Senegal-born Phillis Wheatley's questions— "What pangs excruciating must molest, What sorrows labour in my parent's breast?"—reflect a concern not only for herself but also for her parents, who lost their seven- or eight-year-old daughter to an unknown world.

Once in the Americas, the children picked cotton, suckled tobacco, and weeded crops on plantations and farms, or they served as assistants to housekeepers, seamstresses, artisans, mariners, and merchants. Children learned to perform chores satisfactorily or suffer corporal punishment or other abuse. Parents or "fictive kin"—members of the community not related by blood but who functioned as family—buffered abuses. As William Wells Brown wrote of his mother, "I half forgot the name of slave when she was by my side."

Some slave children ran away. The average runaway was a young male who fled alone, yet there were young females who also became fugitives. An 18th-century newspaper advertised for "a Mulatto, or Quadroon Girl, about 14 years of age, named Seth, but calls herself Sall," reporting that she "sometimes says she is white and often paints her face to cover that deception."

A former slave who was 13 when the Civil War began remembered hearing the Emancipation Proclamation read. "It was a glorious day for us all," she said. Even more glorious was December 18, 1865, the day Congress ratified the 13th Amendment and abolished slavery throughout the United States. Long afterward, Victoria Adams, born a slave, expressed a feeling that so many enslaved children must have shared: "I like being free more better." —*Wilma King, University of Missouri-Columbia*

INCIDENTS IN THE LIFE OF A SLAVE GIRL, by Harriet Jacobs, Boston, 1861. Library Collection.

(OPPOSITE) **REBECCA, AN EMANCIPATED SLAVE, FROM NEW ORLEANS,** photograph by Kimball, 1863. Carte de visite. Prints and Photographs.

(FOLLOWING PAGES) **"THE MODERN MEDEA,"** *Harper's Weekly,* May 18, 1867. Prints and Photographs.

REBECCA, an Emancipated Slave, from New Orleans.

Photographed by KIMBALL, 477 Broadway. N.Y.

THE MODERN MEDEA—THE STORY OF MARGARET GARN

GRAPHED BY BRADY, FROM A PAINTING BY THOMAS NOBLE.—[SEE PAGE 318.]

CHAPTER 4
Antebellum

1786-1861

Sunday. February 17th, 1850

Day fine, pleasant after the morning. Rose as usual washed self and children. Private family devotion. Breakfast. Study. Off to Sab[bath] School, new spelling book and catechisms. After school Church. Preached Pet[er] 5:5 Be clothed with humility. After church called by to see the baby—well. Then home, wrote a note to Bro Slade thanking him for the present of a box of sigars. Then to Bro Carrols for dinner and from there to Capt. [Capitol] Hill to Bro B. Simms funeral, from there to ground to read the Masonic ceremony. Then home. Tea. Went with Bro Fisher to Bro Carrolls, then to 8th St. Pres [Presbyterian] Church & back. Set till 10 then prayer, home at 11, read, wrote, devotion. Retired.

Entry in diary of Rev. John F. Cook

District of Columbia,
County of Washington } to wit.

I Samuel D King, a Justice of the
Peace in and for said County do hereby certify
that I have known the Reverend John F.
Cook for many years as a free man, he having
been born and raised in the city of Washington.

In witness whereof I have hereunto
signed my name & affixed my seal
at the City of Washington this 15th day
of August AD 1842

Sam D King [seal]
JP

[County of Washington] to wit.

... the light colored girl
... known as Mary Victoria
... of the above named
... his wife. also free,

... [hand] & Seal this
... the City of
... D King [seal]
JP

... about ten years of age
... the son of the above named
... free, named Son
... and Seal this 11th day of August
... of Washington
Sam D King JP [seal]

1786-1861 *The antebellum period in America refers to the years between the end of the American Revolution in 1776 and the start of the Civil War in 1861. This period is marked by the establishment of America as an independent nation and the shaping of an American identity. It is also marked by an increase in the pressure to end the slave trade, as the differences between the North and the South become more apparent. Rumors of insurrections by slaves in the Caribbean and in the U.S. led to a tightening of restrictions on the mobility of all Blacks and affected the way of life in both the North and the South. Raids on homes and gatherings of any type were frequent and were sometimes coupled with violence and imprisonment.*

Autobiographies are wonderful firsthand accounts of life in antebellum America, in the North or South. Although shadowed by slavery, Blacks formed communities and established churches, schools, and fraternal societies. Rare documents record marriages, births, and the purchase and sale of land. Printed broadsides, newspapers, and pamphlets provide evidence of the earliest accomplishments of both the enslaved and the free and document early efforts of free Blacks to bring attention to the evils of bondage.

AFRICANS IN AMERICA: THE ANTEBELLUM YEARS

IN 1619 A DUTCH SHIP CAPTAIN brought 20 Africans to work as indentured servants in the new British settlement located in Jamestown, Virginia. Between 1675 and 1695, about 3,000 Africans entered the Chesapeake region alone to be put to work, mostly on the tobacco plantations of Maryland and Virginia. They came from various West African ethnic groups from the region of the Gambia River around the coast to present-day Nigeria. Men and women, whose complexions ranged from brown to black, brought with them numerous languages and customs, including their own African religious beliefs. Occasionally Muslims were among them, and sometimes they came from as far away as Madagascar. Slave owners often commented on their "country markings": scarification on their faces, arms, or torso, for ethnic identity or body ornamentation. Music, drums, and singing frightened whites, who soon outlawed many such African practices, especially drumming. In time, an Africanized English became the language that the Africans and their owners all understood. The Africans received new names. They learned their work and the strict boundaries within which slave life was confined.

By the 18th century, the American colonies were beginning to get a new generation of Africans, born in America, who did not know their parents' homeland. In a few generations, Africa became simply a distant, misunderstood land to most African Americans. With the invention of the cotton gin at the turn of the 19th century, cotton production began to climb and the value of enslaved property

FREE PAPERS WITH TIN HOLDER, Rev. John F. Cook (1842) and daughter Mary Victoria (1844). Cook Family Papers.

expanded exponentially. Cotton production intersected with the growing textile industry in Great Britain and the New England states, leading to revolutionary production rates. Most slaveholders in the South had few slaves, but there were large plantations where hundreds of enslaved Africans worked. By the Civil War, they were producing more cotton than anywhere else in the world. As slave property became increasingly valuable, slaveholders were more strongly determined to protect their right to hold human property. In 1790 African Americans made up about one-fifth of the nation's population. By 1860 four and a half million people of color, enslaved and free, lived in the United States.

FROM THE 17TH CENTURY ON, especially after the American Revolution, a growing free Black population was developing in the United States. African Americans were usually emancipated for diligent work, good conduct, familial connections with their owners, or commendable service. The methods for manumission included court actions, instructions in owners' wills, self-purchase, purchase of one's own family members' freedom with money earned when hired out, governmental decrees, or rewards for military service. State laws declared that children follow the condition of their mother. Thus children born to a free mother were also free.

Free Blacks, especially children, lived under the threat of being sold back into slavery. The states passed laws prohibiting Blacks from assembling or carrying firearms or testifying against whites in court. State governments vacillated about the right of free Blacks to hold and bequeath property, and at various times, state laws prohibited Blacks from reading abolitionist literature, operating boats, obtaining licenses for peddling, participating in certain trades, or having or driving vehicles such as hacks, carts, or drays. Laws also prevented Blacks from aiding runaway slaves.

Free Blacks still formed their own churches, schools, benevolent societies, and businesses. Free persons of color worked as domestics, small farmers, innkeepers, street vendors, ship caulkers, stevedores, sailors and boatmen, draymen, barbers, teamsters, blacksmiths, and liverymen. Blacks purchased their freedom with money earned through skilled labor. Astronomer Benjamin Banneker published an almanac and helped plan the District of Columbia. Preacher Daniel Coker, who published sermons and a diary, became one of the first emigrants to go back to Africa with the American Colonization Society. Despite enslavement, Phillis Wheatley and Jupiter Hammond wrote and published poetry and prose. Absalom Jones and Richard Allen founded churches and benevolent societies. James Forten became rich by manufacturing sails, and Frederick Douglass ably supported himself by abolitionist lectures and journalism. Harriet Tubman tirelessly helped her people as an Underground Railroad conductor and humanitarian, and Frances Ellen Watkins Harper wove plaintive poems.

During the colonial and early national period, some white U.S. statesmen and citizens were uncomfortable with the slave trade, the growing enslaved population, and the expanding number of free people of color throughout the country. In the aftermath of the Revolution, the northern states abolished slavery. Because the free Black population fostered rebellions, harbored runaways, competed with white laborers, lobbied for citizenship rights, and generally sowed discontent among the enslaved, most slave owners resented their presence.

Some leaders began formulating theories for the relocation of free Blacks. Colonization was a volatile issue at antebellum African-American political meetings, which came to be known as the Negro Convention Movement. Frederick Douglass, who saw colonization as rooted in racism and negrophobia, spoke out against it on many occasions. In a *North Star* editorial of January 1849, Douglass lambasted the U.S. Senate about "the wrinkled old 'red herring' of colonization."

"We are of the opinion that the free colored people generally mean to live in America, and not in Africa; and to appropriate a large sum for our removal, would merely be a waste of the public money," Douglass wrote. "We do not mean to go to Liberia.... Here we are, and here we shall remain. While our brethren are in bondage on these shores, it is idle to think of inducing any considerable number of the free colored people to quit this for a foreign land."

The vast majority of Black Americans were adamant about remaining in the U.S. rather than relocating to Africa with the American Colonization Society. They wanted to fight for citizenship rights and emancipation of slaves. Between 12,000 and 18,000 Blacks decided or were forced to emigrate. Most who wanted to return had dual motives: liberation and evangelism. For example, Lott Cary, a preacher from Richmond, Virginia, followed reports about the British Sierra Leone colony and the American Colonization Society. Inspired, Cary determined to immigrate to Liberia in 1820 "to preach to the poor Africans the way of life and salvation." He also uttered a sentiment that would be expressed by other evangelical, literate, or educated free Blacks: "I am an African, and in this country, however meritorious my conduct, and respectable my character, I cannot receive the credit due to either. I wish to go to a country where I shall be estimated by my merits, not by my complexion."

JOHN RUSSWURM, the son of his Jamaican master and a mulatto woman, decided that personal autonomy was impossible for a Black man in the United States. The first Black graduate of Bowdoin College in Maine and the co-founder in 1827 of the first U.S. Black-owned newspaper, *Freedom's Journal*, Russwurm decided to emigrate.

Alexander Crummell, grandson of a West African chief, worked in Liberia for 20 years, from 1853 to 1873. Ordained as a Protestant Episcopal minister and educated at Queens' College, Cambridge, Crummell wrote from Liberia to Black Americans in 1860, saying that all of them should have "some relation to the land of their fathers," whether they emigrated or not. It was "natural," he wrote, "to call upon the children of Africa in foreign lands, to come and participate in the opening treasures of the land of their fathers. Though these treasures are the manifest gift of God to the Negro race, yet that race reaps but the most partial measure of their good advantage." Crummell was not so much encouraging emigration as he was fostering a pan-African community. Many other Black nationalists would echo these sentiments.

During the long night of oppression before the Civil War, African Americans sought liberty. Articulate men and women of color stood in the forefront of the nascent pan-African movement and the abolition struggle. They could not rest until the "land of the free and the home of the brave" declared them "forever free" as well. —*Debra Newman Ham, Morgan State University*

BANNAKER's
NEW-JERSEY, PENNSYLVANIA, DELA-WARE, MARYLAND AND VIRGINIA
ALMANAC,
OR
EPHEMERIS,
FOR THE YEAR OF OUR LORD 1795;
Being the Third after LEAP-YEAR.

HARRY

BANNAKER

BALTIMORE:
PRINTED BY S. & J. ADAMS.

BUILDING AMERICA. Both freedmen and slaves contributed to building the U.S. during the nation's infancy.

In 1791 mathematician and astronomer Benjamin Banneker, born to freed slaves, assisted in surveying the District of Columbia, then known as Federal Territory. From 1792 through 1797 Banneker also published almanacs, which contained practical scientific information such as tide tables, dates of eclipses, and medicinal formulas.

Contributions by slaves to the new nation are often more difficult to identify, since they commonly get attributed to the slaveholder. Henry Baker, an assistant examiner in the U.S. Patent Office, compiled four volumes of patent applications submitted by African Americans up to the early years of the 20th century.

Baker's research helped unearth a number of Black American inventors, including Thomas Jennings, the first African American to receive a patent, who developed a dry cleaning process. Were it not for Baker, Jennings would have been forgotten, because credit for his 1821 patent had been attributed to his owner. On the other hand, Henry Blair, who received a patent in 1834 for his seed planter, was designated a "colored man" in the patent record book.

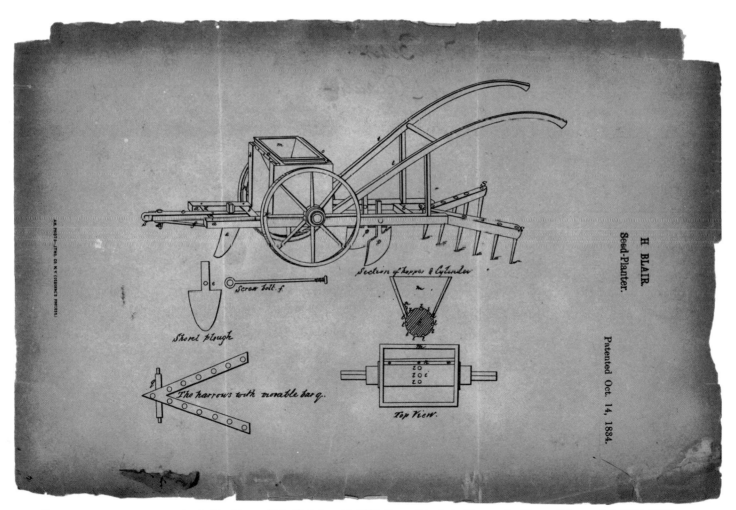

PATENT FOR SEED PLANTER, patented by Henry Blair, October 14, 1834. From *Patents by Negroes,* by Henry Baker, vol. 1, 1834-1887. Library Collection.

(OPPOSITE) **BANNEKER'S ALMANAC,** by Benjamin Banneker, Baltimore, 1795. Library Collection.

This Certifies

That Mr William Graves of Philadelphia
and Miss Catherine T. McCrummell of the same place
were by me united in the bonds of marriage on
the Thirtieth day of May in the year of our
One Thousand Eight Hundred and 49 conformably to the ordinar
of God and the Laws of the State of Pennsylvania

Rev: Wm Douglas

FAMILY AND MARRIAGE. The strength of the Black family was tested during antebellum America. Neither marriages between slaves nor slave families were recognized by American law. That left any semblance of a family susceptible to forcible separation. Slaveholders were free to sell off family members, separating a husband from his wife and children from their mother. Despite the devastation of separation, though, enslaved Blacks formed durable bonds of kinship.

The families of free Blacks, whether living in the South or in the North, also faced restrictions, although they were free to marry legally and to raise families. Traditional wedding ceremonies and baptisms helped to legitimize the Black family as a legal and honorable entity.

MARRIAGE CERTIFICATE BETWEEN WILLIAM GRAVES AND CATHERINE McCRUMMELL, A FREE MAN AND WOMAN, Philadelphia, May 13, 1849. Omnium Gatherum Collection.

WORSHIP SERVICES. Although it was not always easy to do, free Blacks did establish many of their own institutions. They formed social and civic organizations, including benevolent associations, Masonic lodges, and churches. Some, such as the Colored American Institute, founded in 1851, served as a way for Black Americans to celebrate their own accomplishments.

The church in free Black communities was the center of social, intellectual, civic, and economic life. Reacting to racist practices in the white church, former slave Richard Allen founded the African Methodist Episcopal Church in 1816 in Philadelphia. Allen became the denomination's first bishop.

On the plantation, the Bible could be used by both sides of the conflict. It was quoted both to justify slavery and to justify liberation and freedom. Congregations in the South often included worshipers of both races, although the congregation was segregated by seating arrangement and rarely was a Black preacher engaged. Black believers often held their own secret worship services in the woods.

(OPPOSITE) **RICHARD ALLEN,** artist unknown, 1784. Chalk and pastel portrait. General Museum Collection.

MEDAL AWARDED TO ARTIST DAVID BUSTILL BOWSER BY THE COLORED AMERICAN INSTITUTE, 1851. David Bustill Bowser Collection.

(BELOW) **"FAMILY WORSHIP IN A PLANTATION, SOUTH CAROLINA,"** *The Illustrated London News,* December 1863. Prints and Photographs.

FAMILY WORSHIP IN A PLANTATION IN SOUTH CAROLINA.—SEE PAGE 574

"Office of the Fred'k Douglass Papers and The North Star," printed in *Frederick Douglass: The Orator,* by James Monroe Gregory, Springfield, Massachusetts, 1893. Library Collection.

THE BLACK PRESS IN ANTEBELLUM AMERICA

AFRICAN-AMERICAN FREEMEN EMBRACED the ideals of civil liberty and equality of opportunity in America from the earliest days of the Revolutionary War. Some, such as Crispus Attucks, gave their lives in pursuit of the objectives that gave birth to the new nation. In 1787 two Black clergymen, Richard Allen and Absalom Jones, led the first nonviolent public demonstration against racial discrimination in America. Over the next three decades, Black citizens sought to attain the "inalienable rights" that had been set forth in Thomas Jefferson's declaration using various means, including petitions to Congress and resolutions enacted by a mass public meeting held in Philadelphia.

Throughout the antebellum period the traditional newspaper press generally denied Black citizens access to their columns, and some routinely castigated Black citizens. By 1827 it was clear to Richard Allen and other prominent free Black men who lived in the northeastern seaboard states that the time had come to launch a newspaper to "plead our own cause." *Freedom's Journal* was the product of a meeting held in New York City of clergymen, businessmen, and other African-American community leaders.

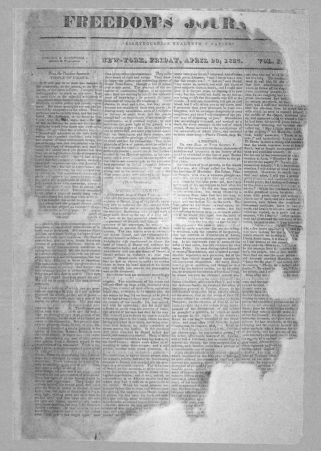

Published weekly for two years under the co-editorship of the Rev. Samuel Cornish and John B. Russwurm, *Freedom's Journal* inspired other newspapers and periodicals. Among them were David Walker's strident pamphlet *Walker's Appeal*, published in Boston in 1829, and *Mirror of Liberty*, the first Black magazine, produced by David Ruggles in New York in 1837. The growth of antebellum Black newspapers soon paralleled the westward expansion of the United States. Black newspapers appeared in Ohio, Michigan, and Kansas well before the onset of the Civil War.

Perhaps the most influential paper to appear during the final two decades of antebellum America was Frederick Douglass's *North Star*, founded in Rochester, New York, in 1847. Douglass and his writings had been a staple of the white-owned abolitionist paper *The Liberator*, which began under the editorship of William Lloyd Garrison in 1831. Douglass founded the *North Star*—named in recognition of the celestial body used by runaway slaves to navigate their freedom—to show that African Americans could best further their cause through publications that they independently owned and operated. *North Star* published continuously for 16 years but was renamed *Frederick Douglass's Paper* following a merger in 1851. —*Clint C. Wilson II, Howard University*

FREEDOM'S JOURNAL, edited by Samuel E. Cornish and John B. Russwurm, March 16, 1827. First issue. General Museum Collection.

An ELEGIAC
POEM,

On the DEATH of that celebrated Divine, and eminent Servant of JESUS CHRIST, the late Reverend, and pious

GEORGE WHITEFIELD,

Chaplain to the Right Honourable the Countess of HUNTINGDON, &c. &c.

Who made his Exit from this transitory State, to dwell in the celestial Realms of

Bliss, on LORD's-Day, 30th of September, 1770, when he was seiz'd with a Fit of the Asthma, at NEWBURY-PORT, near BOSTON, in NEW-ENGLAND. In which is a Condolatory Address to His truly noble Benefactress the worthy and pious Lady HUNTINGDON,---and the Orphan-Children in GEORGIA ; who, with many Thousands, are left, by the Death of this great Man, to lament the Loss of a Father, Friend, and Benefactor.

By PHILLIS, a Servant Girl of 17 Years of Age, belonging to Mr. J. WHEATLEY, of BOSTON :---And has been but 9 Years in this Country from Africa.

HAIL happy Saint on thy immortal throne !
　To thee complaints of grievance are unknown ;
We hear no more the music of thy tongue,
Thy wonted auditories cease to throng.
Thy lessons in unequal'd accents flow'd !
While emulation in each bosom glow'd ;
Thou didst, in strains of eloquence refin'd,
Inflame the soul, and captivate the mind.
Unhappy we, the setting Sun deplore !
Which once was splendid, but it shines no more ;
He leaves this earth for Heaven's unmeasur'd height :
And worlds unknown, receive him from our sight ;
There WHITEFIELD wings, with rapid course his way,
And sails to Zion, through vast seas of day.

　When his AMERICANS were burden'd sore,
When streets were crimson'd with their guiltless gore !
Unrival'd friendship in his breast now strove :
The fruit thereof was charity and love
Towards America-----couldst thou do more
Than leave thy native home, the British shore,
To cross the great Atlantic's wat'ry road,
To see America's distress'd abode ?
Thy prayers, great Saint, and thy incessant cries,
Have pierc'd the bosom of thy native skies !
Thou moon hast seen, and ye bright stars of light
Have witness been of his requests by night !
He pray'd that grace in every heart might dwell :
He long'd to see America excell ;
He charg'd its youth to let the grace divine
Arise, and in their future actions shine ;
He offer'd THAT he did himself receive,

A greater gift not GOD himself can give :
He urg'd the need of HIM to every one ;
It was no less than GOD's co-equal SON !
Take HIM ye wretched for your only good ;
Take HIM ye starving-souls to be your food.
Ye thirsty, come to this life giving stream :
Ye Preachers, take him for your joyful theme ;
Take HIM, " my dear AMERICANS," he said,
Be your complaints in his kind bosom laid :
Take HIM ye Africans, he longs for you ;
Impartial SAVIOUR, is his title due ;
If you will chuse to walk in grace's road,
You shall be sons, and kings, and priests to GOD.

　Great COUNTESS ! we Americans revere
Thy name, and thus condole thy grief sincere :
We mourn with thee, that TOMB obscurely plac'd,
In which thy Chaplain undisturb'd doth rest.
New-England sure, doth feel the ORPHAN's smart ;
Reveals the true sensations of his heart :
Since this fair Sun, withdraws his golden rays,
No more to brighten these distressful days !
His lonely Tabernacle, sees no more
A WHITEFIELD landing on the British shore :
Then let us view him in yon azure skies :
Let every mind with this lov'd object rise.
No more can he exert his lab'ring breath,
Seiz'd by the cruel messenger of death.
What can his dear AMERICA return ?
But drop a tear upon his happy urn,
Thou tomb, shalt safe retain thy sacred trust,
Till life divine re-animate his dust.

Sold by EZEKIEL RUSSELL, in Queen-Street, and JOHN BOYLES, in Marlboro'-Street.

PHILLIS WHEATLEY. Phillis Wheatley, the first published African-American poet, was born in Senegal in about 1753. At the age of seven, she was captured and sold into slavery to Boston merchant John Wheatley, as a servant girl to his wife. A bright and willing learner, Wheatley was taught to read and write. She was also versed in Greek and Latin classics, plus history, astronomy, geography, and literature.

Her first poem, titled "On Mssers. Hussey and Coffin," appeared in 1767 in the *Newport Mercury*, a Rhode Island newspaper. The publication of a poetic tribute on the death of evangelical preacher George Whitefield in 1770 brought Wheatley widespread recognition in Boston.

Although her poems continued to appear in various publications from 1771 to 1773, no one in the Boston area would publish her book of poetry. With help from a family friend, the volume *Poems on Various Subjects, Religious and Moral* was finally published in London in 1773. This book earned Wheatley attention both in the United States and abroad.

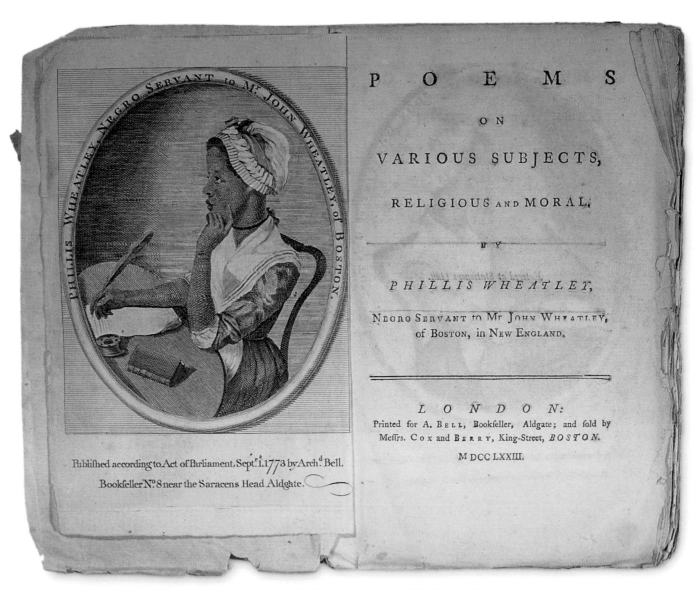

POEMS ON VARIOUS SUBJECTS, RELIGIOUS AND MORAL, by Phillis Wheatley, London, 1773. Library Collection.

(OPPOSITE) **"AN ELEGIAC POEM, ON THE DEATH OF...GEORGE WHITEFIELD,"** by Phillis Wheatley, 1770. General Museum Collection.

CHAPTER 5
Runaways, Rebellions, Abolitionism
1700-1865

I had seen Robert, prior to this, at my father's house, and he had requested me to tell him the route, because he said I understood the geography of the country…. I asked him if he knew what the consequence of giving such information would be, if known. He answered in the negative. I said, suppose you are caught in the attempt to escape, you would certainly be interrogated as to the person from whom you gained your information, and if you were to say you obtained the knowledge from me, according to law, I would be imprisoned for the long term of ninety-nine years.

To this Robert replied, nearly, in these words, "If you will only tell me how I may escape, I will promise, in the sight of God, that I will suffer my life to be taken before I will inform against you."

I said, it is enough; I believe you.

Rev. William Troy, 1861
"The Escape of Robert Blackburn, and Great Struggle for Liberty," from *Hair-Breadth Escapes from Slavery to Freedom*

AM I NOT A MAN AND A BROTHER?

ADDRESS FROM THE SLAVES OF THE BRITISH SUGAR COLONIES, TO THE PEOPLE OF ENGLAND.

GOOD WHITE PEOPLE OF ENGLAND,

We have heard with feelings of gratitude, that you have Petitioned your King and Government, that we might be relieved from the cruel oppression under which we suffer. We sincerely thank you for your benevolent exertions, and we have no doubt but they will be blessed by Him who said, when he sent Moses to deliver the Israelites, "I have surely seen the affliction of my people which are in Egypt, and have heard their cry, by reason of their task-masters." We know that our masters, who "use our service without wages," are many of them much more miserable than we are, and are very generally embarrassed in their circumstances—for oppression seldom prospers, even in this life.

It would be better for them, as well as for us and for you, if slavery was abolished. We would work willingly for wages, without drivers behind us; and we would live peaceably with the white people, and not injure any one.

You are now obliged to pay millions of pounds every year; and many thousands of lives are lost, by keeping soldiers in the West Indies, in order to prevent us from rising against our masters. All this would be saved to you. You are also obliged to pay a higher duty on all Sugar, &c. raised by free people, than on that which is raised by slaves; and you pay our masters a bounty when they export Sugar from England; by which means you enable them to bear the expense of keeping us in bondage, and your Sugar costs you much more than it otherwise would.

If your Government will not therefore listen to your prayers on our behalf, there is still one way by which you can abolish our slavery.—*Leave off using all articles which are produced by the labour of slaves, as much as you can, particularly* WEST INDIA AND MAURITIUS SUGAR; *this article is the principal cause of our oppressive labour*. You might procure plenty of Sugar at a much cheaper rate, made by free men in Asia; or you might induce the natives of Africa to raise it in their own country, which would produce it abundantly.

You may thus easily break our chains—
Relieve yourselves from oppressive burdens—
And wash your hands from our blood!

1700-1865

African peoples have consistently resisted their enslavement during every stage of the process, beginning with their capture in Africa and extending through their enslavement in Europe and the Americas. Sometimes they resisted to the death. Battles were staged on several levels and carried out both individually and collectively. While enslaved Africans were in the forefront of efforts to cast off the yokes of slavery, pressure was also applied by white abolitionists, free Blacks, and escaped slaves. Antislavery pamphlets, published accounts of acts of cruelty, and impassioned broadsides generated public support for antislavery efforts on both sides of the Atlantic. Free Blacks used the pulpit, their own newspapers, and organizations to tell of their own experiences and fight to end slavery. Enslaved persons exercised daily control over their situation simply by faking illness, committing arson, escaping, or helping others to escape through the Underground Railroad. Fear of slave revolts was justified following the slave revolution in Haiti and Gabriel Prosser's rebellion in Richmond, Virginia, in August 1800. Such efforts first challenged slave trafficking across the Atlantic and finally concentrated on ending slavery in the Western Hemisphere.

Pathway to Freedom: The Underground Railroad

The history of the Underground Railroad is a tribute to the human spirit and the desire to be free. It illustrates the lengths people will go to in order to gain greater control over their lives and provide a better future for their families. It also highlights the willingness of principled people to aid others embarked on their journey to self-determination. All of the individuals involved in this endeavor understood the jeopardy in which they placed themselves and their families. But they accepted the danger because they believed that freedom was the right of everyone, not just of a privileged few. They also believed in the end that freedom was worth whatever risks and sacrifices one needed to take to attain it or make it available to others.

Unraveling the network that constituted the Underground Railroad is not a simple task. Essentially, it was a very loosely organized system. Secrecy was a critical part of its successful operation, along with varying patterns of operation depending on the region where it functioned. Most participants followed one of three major pathways out of slavery to northern states or Canada. One route traveled along the Atlantic seaboard through Washington, Philadelphia, New York, and Boston. A second moved along the Ohio River Valley through the states of Ohio and Indiana to Detroit or through Buffalo to Canada. The third route followed the Mississippi River to cities like St. Louis and Chicago. Other routes took travelers south to Mexico or into the swamps of Florida. Embedded in

"Am I Not a Man and a Brother? Address from the Slaves of the British Sugar Colonies, to the People of England," before 1833. Broadside. Prints and Photographs.

each of these routes were people both enslaved and free, who stood willing to provide help to those brave individuals seeking freedom.

A diversity of people participated in the Underground Railroad enterprise. It was one of the first interracial activist movements in the nation, attracting people from a variety of racial groups, religious affiliations, economic classes, and geographic regions. What united them was their abiding belief in freedom. The desire to make freedom universally accessible motivated all of the participants, regardless of what role they played in the endeavor.

THE MOST IMPORTANT PLAYERS IN THIS STORY were the enslaved African Americans who made the decision to run away and seek liberty. Without them, the Underground Railroad would not have existed. They defied their slave masters, the law, and the odds with the hope of success and a better life. All types of people fled slavery, though most often they were younger than 30, traveling alone, and male. Names like Frederick Douglass, who became a nationally recognized abolitionist speaker, Harriet Jacobs, Henry "Box" Brown, William and Ellen Craft, Henry Long, and Anthony Burns come to mind when identifying individuals who had the temerity to risk life and limb in the hope of a better future.

Those who fled did not make this decision lightly, as failure had dire consequences. Imprisonment, whipping, branding, sale farther south, and death—all condoned by southern legal systems—awaited any freedom-seeker recaptured and returned. Newspaper articles, court records, and runaway slave advertisements all bear witness to the punishments that recaptured runaways might expect. Reaching the North did not guarantee success, either, as statutes like the Fugitive Slave Law of 1850 enlisted northern authorities in the effort to return runaways. Both Henry Long and Anthony Burns were recaptured and returned south despite the best efforts of their supporters to prevent this from happening.

But for those who escaped successfully, a new life awaited. As William Wells Brown described it, "The fact that I was a freeman—could walk, talk, eat and sleep, as a man and no one to stand over me with the blood-clotted cowhide—all this made me feel that I was not myself." Freedom created a new person with new options and a new destiny. The rewards at the end of the journey made the dangers worth the effort.

FOR MANY RUNNING AWAY, the chances for success increased if they connected with others who could provide help in a variety of ways. In particular, if they found someone to escort them on their journey or who stepped forward to help them as they reached free soil, they would be much better off. Many times these so-called conductors, who traveled south and brought people north, were African Americans themselves. They frequently were individuals who themselves had escaped slavery and now returned to aid others. The best known of these individuals was Harriet Tubman, who returned south 19 times to help family and friends escape. As legend has it, Tubman never lost a single passenger. She frustrated southern authorities because of their inability to stop or capture her. John Parker of Ripley, Ohio, returned regularly to Kentucky to help runaways reach and cross the Ohio River, which marked the border between slave territory and free states. He made this trip routinely for more than a decade, and in the process helped hundreds of people gain their freedom. Others who performed similar feats included Josiah Henson, Elijah Anderson, and white conductors such as Calvin Fairbank, Seth Concklin, and John Fairfield. All of them put themselves in personal danger because of their disdain for the institution of slavery and the manner in which it degraded human dignity.

Once runaways reached free soil, the underground network became more active and helpful. Stationmasters located in small towns, villages, solitary homes, and large cities alike stood ready to provide food, shelter, clothing, and guidance for escaped freedom-seekers. African Americans again were key to this network: From the very beginning, they made themselves and their homes available. Some scholars have argued they were the first line of help in the North, in part because enslaved African Americans on the run had to remain ever cautious and felt safer approaching another African American when they entered a strange environment. Levi Coffin, often referred to as the "president" of the Underground Railroad, pointed out that many times he only learned after the fact about runaways who had passed through, because the African-American community had already taken care of everything.

TO OPERATE SUCCESSFULLY, the system had to rely upon a wide variety of people who stood ready to help. In Delaware, Thomas Garret was an important participant. He was convicted of aiding the escape of a fugitive family and heavily fined for his actions. His defiant response in the courtroom was to say that he considered the penalty imposed on him as a license to help fugitive slaves for the rest of his life. Garret usually sent the individuals he aided on to another ally, William Still, a freedman who worked with the Pennsylvania Society for the Abolition of Slavery. After recording their story, Still connected the newly free slaves with others in the chain that stretched to Boston, upstate New York, and Canada. It was an effective system that enabled hundreds of individuals to reach freedom successfully. In other parts of the country, similar networks also existed to support freedom-seekers, operated by people who offered assistance despite the dangers.

The ultimate goal of the Underground Railroad was to bring an end to slavery. The individuals who were active in the system believed that slavery was incongruous with the lofty principles of the founding documents of this nation. Consequently, enslaved African Americans seeking freedom and sympathetic individuals from multiple backgrounds scattered across the nation worked together to undermine slavery and its grip on the nation. Their efforts were extraordinary, praiseworthy, and ultimately successful. They played an important part in awakening the conscience of the nation against the evils of slavery, an important issue in the Civil War and an impetus behind the passage of the 13th Amendment to the Constitution. In light of these results, the Underground Railroad was certainly one of the most significant activist movements in the United States during the first half of the 19th century. —*Spencer R. Crew, National Underground Railroad Freedom Center*

ORGANIZED ESCAPES. The Underground Railroad was an organized network of people, both Black and white, who helped runaway slaves escape. Most estimates claim that at least 100,000 persons escaped during the first half of the 19th century, the majority between 1830 and 1865, the years when the Underground Railroad operated. The vocabulary that developed to talk about Underground Railroad escapes was influenced by steam railroad travel, newly developing at the time. The "conductor" moved the fugitives north, allowing them to stop to rest and eat at "stations" or "depots" before they continued along the "railroad" north. Flight was dangerous. Fugitives feared recapture and subsequent punishment. Anyone assisting escapees could be jailed.

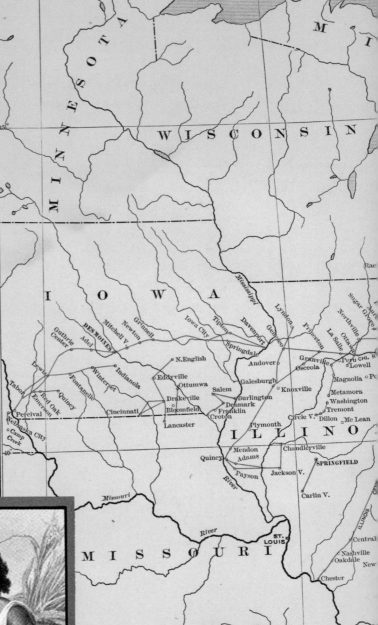

"THE HUNTED SLAVES," by C. G. Lewis, 1865. Engraving based on a painting of the same name by Richard Ansdell, 1861. General Museum Collection.

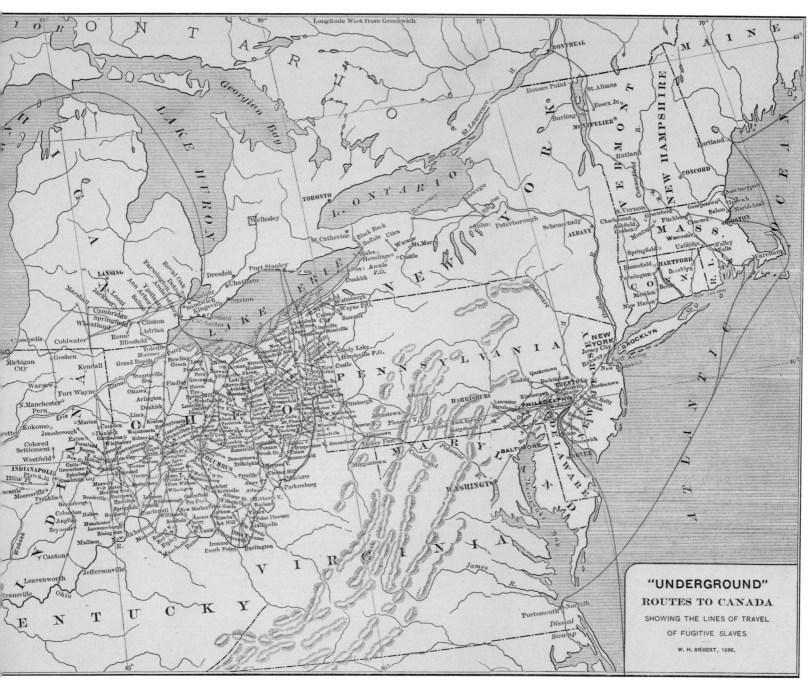

"UNDERGROUND" ROUTES TO CANADA, map printed in *The Underground Railroad: From Slavery to Freedom*, by Wilbur Henry Siebert, New York, 1898. Omnium Gatherum Collection.

TOUSSAINT LOUVERTURE

TOUSSAINT AND REVOLUTION. Blacks enslaved on the coffee and sugar plantations of Haiti, a French colony on the western half of the huge island of Hispaniola, endured some of the worst conditions of any slaves of the Western Hemisphere.

On August 22, 1791, more than 100,000 slaves revolted against the French planters, who were vastly outnumbered by them. This marked the beginning of the Haitian war of independence.

François Dominique Toussaint L'Ouverture was 50 years old when the revolution began. He advanced in military leadership as the revolution proceeded. Allying with France in 1801 to defend Haiti from contending European forces, both British and Spanish, Toussaint conquered Santo Domingo, on Hispaniola's southern coast, proclaimed himself governor, and declared an end to slavery. He retired from public life in 1802 but was soon arrested and sent to France, where seven months later he died of pneumonia in prison.

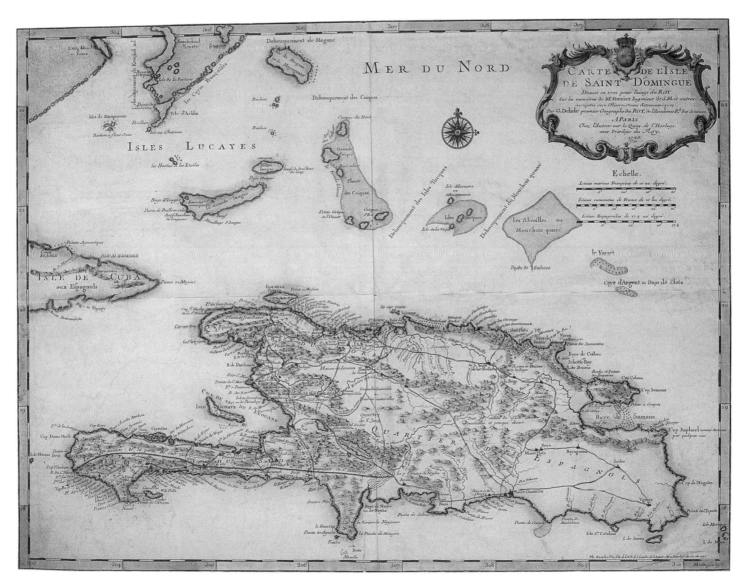

"CARTE DE L'ISLE DE SAINT DOMINGUE," map by Guillaume Delisle, 1725. Cartographic Collection.

(OPPOSITE) **TOUSSAINT L'OUVERTURE**, 1939. Color postcard printed on the anniversary of the French Revolution by the Société des Amis L'Abbé Grégoire, based on a French engraving from 1802. Prints and Photographs.

THE CHURCH'S ROLE IN 19TH-CENTURY ABOLITION

THE 19TH CENTURY IN AMERICAN HISTORY was fraught with conflicting ideas and images. The American Christian church embodied these diametrically opposed views, from every facet of society and in areas of race, gender, and class. Enslaved worshipers initiated the Black church in "hush harbors"—places where slaves could worship in secret. The church's spread to early southern Baptists, and the genesis of the African Methodist Episcopal (A.M.E.) denomination, demonstrated the desire of African people to seek fellowship with each other and find communion with God, free and unrestrained.

African-American abolitionist and antislavery movements were integral parts of the Black church's theology. Christian leaders such as Henry Highland Garnet, Richard Allen, Sojourner Truth, and Frederick Douglass were all former slaves, and they sought to see an end to slavery. The risk of speaking out was a personal sacrifice few took in light of the potentially dangerous outcome. The Black church provided visibility, an extended family network, and interdenominational ties that ensured that no threat would go unchallenged.

The level of pressure the Black church placed on society varied in its intensity. There were antislavery rallies, powerful orators, and subversion through the Underground Railroad, books, and newspapers. In particular, the use of the print media was an instrumental aspect of the Black church's rebellion against slavery. By capturing and publishing the narratives of escaped persons, as well as selling the stories of famous persons, Black churches generated the capital needed to continue the intense struggle to end slavery in America.

The abolitionist and antislavery movement organized around the A.M.E. Church because the church was located in Philadelphia and its leadership was a composite of the freeborn and ex-slaves. The A.M.E. pulpit served as an abolitionists' platform, from which all African-American Christians were welcomed to address exclusively Black congregations without scorn or rejection.

Notable protest came from the A.M.E. Church on the East Coast, but there were other African-American Christians who spoke out as well. Israel Campbell, a former slave and Baptist from Texas, lamented in his autobiography about his lot during slavery: "I was born a slave, saw both the bright and the gloomy sides of the institution, suffered its bitter sorrows....Three of my children are yet [enslaved]....Would God approve of such hypocrisy in one whose mission is to preach peace and truth? I think God has pointed out the only just way," Campbell wrote. He believed God asked for all to contribute by "rescuing many from bondage." —*Ida E. Jones, Moorland-Spingarn Research Center*

HENRY HIGHLAND GARNET, photograph by Rockwood & Co., 1860s. Gregoria Frasier Goins Papers.

(OPPOSITE) **JARENA LEE, FRONTISPIECE FROM** *RELIGIOUS EXPERIENCE AND JOURNAL OF MRS. JARENA LEE,* by Jarena Lee, Philadelphia, 1849. Library Collection.

BLACK ABOLITIONISTS. The abolitionist movement in America is customarily dated from the publication of the *Liberator*, an antislavery newspaper founded and edited by William Lloyd Garrison that first appeared January 1, 1831. "I am in earnest—I will not equivocate—I will not excuse—I will not retreat a single inch—AND I WILL BE HEARD," wrote Garrison in the first issue.

Among the rising militant voices were Black abolitionists who argued for the end of slavery and demanded that Blacks be viewed as equal citizens. Free Black citizens like David Walker and runaway slaves such as Henry Highland Garnet and Frederick Douglass wrote and lectured about the injustice of enslavement. Women—including Frances Ellen Watkins Harper, Lucretia Coffin Mott, and sisters Angelina and Sarah Grimké—were equally outspoken. This period is chronicled vividly in the personal papers of abolitionists and in antislavery writings collected and published by Lewis Tappan.

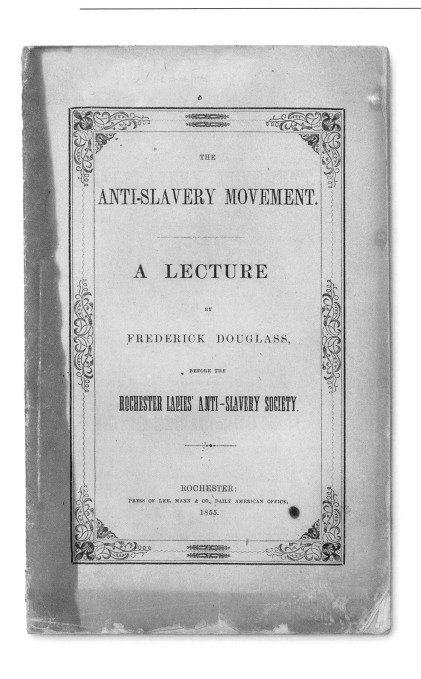

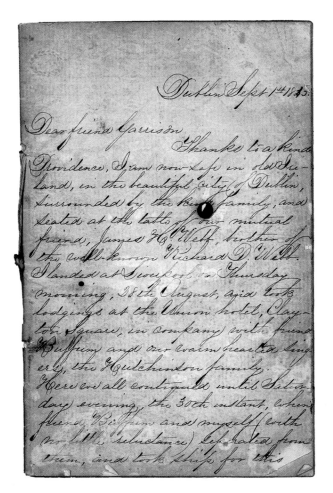

LETTER FROM FREDERICK DOUGLASS TO WILLIAM LLOYD GARRISON, September 1, 1845. Frederick Douglass Collection.

(LEFT) **"THE ANTI-SLAVERY MOVEMENT,"** program of a lecture presented by Frederick Douglass, Rochester, New York, 1855. Frederick Douglass Collection.

(OPPOSITE) **FREDERICK DOUGLASS,** photographer unknown, ca 1850. Daguerreotype mounted in brass frame and mat. Frederick Douglass Collection, Howard University Museum.

CHAPTER 6
The Civil War
1861-1865

The first suits worn by the boys were red coats and pants, which they disliked very much, for, they said, "The rebels see us, miles away." The first colored troops did not receive any pay for eighteen months, and the men had to depend wholly on what they received from the commissary, established by General Saxton. A great many of these men had large families, and as they had no money to give them, their wives were obliged to support themselves and children by washing for the officers of the gunboats and the soldiers, and making cakes and pies which they sold to the boys in camp. Finally, in 1863, the government decided to give them half pay, but the men would not accept this. They wanted "full pay" or nothing. They preferred rather to give their services to the state, which they did until 1864, when the government granted them full pay, with all the back pay due.

Susie King Taylor, 1902
Reminiscences of My Life in Camp
with the 33d United States Colored Troops
Late 1st S.C. Volunteers

MEN OF COLOR, TO ARMS!

A Call by Frederick Douglass.

When first the Rebel cannon shattered the walls of Sumter, and drove away its starving garrison, I predicted that the war then and there inaugurated would not be fought out entirely by white men. Every month's experience during these two dreary years has confirmed that opinion. A war undertaken and brazenly carried on for the perpetual enslavement of colored men, calls logically and loudly upon colored men to help to suppress it. Only a moderate share of sagacity was needed to see that the arm of the slave was the best defence against the arm of the slaveholder. Hence with every reverse to the National arms, with every exulting shout of victory raised by the slaveholding Rebels, I have implored the imperilled nation to unchain against her foes her powerful black hand. Slowly and reluctantly that appeal is beginning to be heeded. Stop not now to complain that it was not heeded sooner. It may, or it may not have been best—that it should not. This is not the time to discuss that question. Leave it to the future. When the war is over, the country is saved, peace is established, and the black man's rights are secured, as they will be, history with an impartial hand, will dispose of that and sundry other questions. Action! action! not criticism, is the plain duty of this hour. Words are now useful only as they stimulate to blows. The office of speech now is only to point out when, where and how to strike to the best advantage. There is no time for delay. The tide is at flood that leads on to fortune. From east to west, from north to south the sky is written all over with "now or never." Liberty won by white men would lack half its lustre. Who would be free themselves must strike the blow. Better even to die free than to live slaves. This is the sentiment of every brave colored man among us. There are weak and cowardly men in all nations. We have them among us. They will tell you that this is the "whiteman's war;" that you will be "better off after than before the war;" that the getting of you into the army is to "sacrifice you on the first opportunity." Believe them not—cowards themselves, they do not wish to have their cowardice shamed by your brave example. Leave them to their timidity, or to whatever other motive may hold them back.

I have not thought lightly of the words I am now addressing to you. The counsel I give comes of close observation of the great struggle now in progress—and of the deep conviction that this is your hour and mine.

In good earnest, then, and after the best deliberation, I, now, for the first time during the war, feel at liberty to call and counsel you to arms. By every consideration which binds you to your enslaved fellow countrymen, and the peace and welfare of your country; by every aspiration which you cherish for the freedom and equality of yourselves and your children; by all the ties of blood and identity which make us one with the brave black men now fighting our battles in Louisiana, in South Carolina, I urge you to fly to arms, and smite with death the power that would bury the Government and your liberty in the same hopeless grave. I wish I could tell you that the State of New York calls you to this high honor. For the moment her constituted authorities are silent on the subject. They will speak by and by, and doubtless on the right side; but we are not compelled to wait for her. We can get at the throat of treason and Slavery through the State of Massachusetts.

She was first in the war of Independence; first to break the chains of her slaves; first to make the black man equal before the law; first to admit colored children to her common schools, and she was the first to answer with her blood the alarm cry of the nation—when its capital was menaced by rebels. You know her patriotic Governor, and you know Charles Sumner—I need add no more.

Massachusetts now welcomes you to arms as her soldiers. She has but a small colored population from which to recruit. She has full leave of the General Government to send one regiment to the war, and she has undertaken to do it. Go quickly and help fill up this first colored regiment from the North. I am authorized to assure you that you will receive the same wages, the same rations, the same equipments, the same protection, the same treatment and the same bounty secured to white soldiers. You will be led by able and skillful officers—men who will take especial pride in your efficiency and success. They will be quick to accord to you all the honor you shall merit by your valor—and see that your rights and feelings are respected by other soldiers. I have assured myself on these points—and can speak with authority. More than twenty years unswerving devotion to our common cause, may give me some humble claim to be trusted at this momentous crisis.

I will not argue. To do so implies hesitation and doubt, and you do not hesitate. You do not doubt. The day dawns—the morning star is bright upon the horizon! The iron gate of our prison stands half open. One gallant rush from the North will fling it wide open, while four millions of our brothers and sisters shall march out into Liberty! The chance is now given you to end in a day the bondage of centuries, and to rise in one bound from social degradation to the plane of common equality with all other varieties of men. Remember Denmark Vesey of Charleston. Remember Nathaniel Turner of South Hampton; remember Shields, Green, and Copeland, who followed noble John Brown, and fell as glorious martyrs for the cause of the slaves. Remember that in a contest with oppression, the Almighty has no attribute which can take sides with oppressors. The case is before you. This is our golden opportunity—let us accept it—and forever wipe out the dark reproaches unsparingly hurled against us by our enemies. Win for ourselves the gratitude of our country—and the best blessings of our posterity through all time. The nucleus of this first regiment is now in camp at Readville, a short distance from Boston. I will undertake to forward to Boston all persons adjudged fit to be mustered into this regiment, who shall apply to me at any time within the next two weeks.

FREDERICK DOUGLASS.

Rochester, March 2, 1863.

1861-1865 *During the War Between the States, Black people participated on many levels. After President Lincoln signed the Emancipation Proclamation, Black men could officially participate in the war as soldiers. Throughout the war, a total of more than 186,000 Black soldiers are estimated to have fought as part of the Union Army, including 93,000 from Confederate states, 40,000 from the border slave states, and 53,000 from the free states. By the close of the war, 38,000 had given their lives to end 250 years of slavery in America. Slaves and free Blacks also served in the Confederate Army, working as blacksmiths, cooks, chaplains, and laborers. Not until March 1865, though, two months before the war ended, did the Confederacy allow Blacks to serve as soldiers.*

The historical documents generated during the Civil War illustrate the Black experience as active participants. Clothing account books, pension records, and enlistment records provide information on military life but also shed light on personal matters such as marriage and income. Published accounts, particularly those of women, describe military life as well as the contributions of nurses and teachers to the war effort.

THE ERA OF THE CIVIL WAR

AMONG TRANSFORMATIVE EVENTS IN AMERICAN HISTORY, none figures more prominently than the Civil War. As the North and South fought to defend their respective definitions of liberty and nationhood, the bloody struggle irrevocably altered the lives of many of the more than 30 million Americans who chose sides, some of whom shouldered arms against their own brothers. Eventually, more than 600,000 Americans would die on battlefields or as a consequence of the squalor and disease that was prevalent within military and prisoner-of-war camps. Many more would be disabled by the weaponry that was arrayed on either side. Women would have thrust upon them premature widowhood, and children would grow up never experiencing paternal affection. Fortunes would be lost as property was destroyed or was appropriated by the enemy. And an agrarian way of life would be altered by new labor arrangements and by the assault on the supremacy of the planter class.

But no transformation compared with the conversion in legal status of four million enslaved men and women from chattel to human beings. Bondage had kept them perpetually at labor and had denied them the basic rights and privileges of membership in the human family. The war became their salvation, an instrument of liberation that enabled them, finally, to claim an American birthright.

"MEN OF COLOR, TO ARMS!" by Frederick Douglass, March 2, 1863. Broadside. Frederick Douglass Collection.

From the beginning of the conflict, African Americans in both the ostensibly free North and the slaveholding South recognized the war's potential to further the cause of freedom. While white men and women debated esoteric issues of states' rights versus national prerogative, Black men and women were motivated to action by considerations that were more practical. They sought freedom not in its abstract form, but rather in ways that were meant to overturn the many daily proscriptions to their lives.

To the enslaved, freedom meant unencumbered physical mobility; they expected to be able to relocate to wherever they wished, whenever the need or desire arose. Freedom meant economic autonomy, or at the least, compensated employment. The enslaved anticipated that release from bondage would permit unimpeded acquisition of education for themselves and their children, legal recognition of their marriages, and authority over and protection of their families. They expected full citizenship rights, and the exercise of a political voice by voting and holding public office. In short, freedom meant the enjoyment of the same privileges as those of other Americans and the right to live dignified and self-directed lives.

THE QUEST FOR STATUTORY AND PERSONAL FREEDOM led African-American men and women to champion the Union cause. They formed themselves into military units and drilled in anticipation of being mustered into the Union forces. Black leaders urged the North to expand its goal, which until September 1862 was preservation of the Union.

But, eager to end the conflict with a minimum of disruption to America's domestic institutions, including slavery, the Lincoln Administration and the northern people determined that African Americans would be kept at the periphery of the struggle and that Black freedom would be delayed. African-American calls for emancipation of the enslaved were ignored, and offers to enter the fight were rebuffed, even as Union defeats mounted.

Finally, after more than a year of war, President Lincoln acquiesced by making the conflict one that had as a goal the demise of slavery in those areas that were still under the control of Confederate forces. Although the proclamation was defined narrowly, African Americans still welcomed it, believing, as Frederick Douglass had predicted, that once freedom had been proclaimed in one part of the South, slavery could not survive in the rest. Indeed, the Emancipation Proclamation eventually led to the passage of the 13th Amendment, which ended the practice of slavery throughout the nation.

Lincoln's Emancipation Proclamation also enabled Black men to don the Union blue and enter military service. At Port Hudson in Louisiana, at Milliken's Bend in Missisippi, at Morris Island in South Carolina, and in many other places that are long forgotten, Black men fought valiantly in defense of the nation and in support of freedom. Ultimately more than 186,000 black men, drawn from both the North and the South, enslaved and free, served the Union cause; 38,000 lost their lives in the struggle.

As military men won victories on the battlefield, Black civilians lent their support and pressed the cause of freedom on the home front. In the North, they helped to fund efforts to aid the many destitute freed people and provided relief to soldiers' families. Free men and women also continued to agitate for expansion of the limited liberties that they had been accorded since the abolition of northern slavery. They demanded equal political participation; they insisted on the removal of laws that prohibited immigration and excluded testimony from Black witnesses in cases involving white men; and they sought an end to the practice of segregation in public transportation.

Most free Black men and women in the South followed a more cautious path than those in the North. It was characterized by feigned outward loyalty to the Confederacy along with clandestine dedication to the success of the Union that turned into action whenever the opportunity presented itself. As Union troops advanced, Black men and women provided them with military intelligence and dared even to smuggle Union sympathizers and soldiers trapped behind enemy lines to safety.

THE ENSLAVED PEOPLE THEMSELVES were hardly a helpless assemblage waiting to be rescued and whisked away to freedom. Even before the North embraced the idea of emancipation, enslaved blacks had seized their freedom by escaping plantation and farm. Those who remained behind by choice or circumstance worked to destroy slavery from within. They challenged the traditional relationship between owner and owned, refusing to stay at their labors and being general irritants in the estimation of those whites left behind to control them. Even in areas that were not touched by the provisions of the Emancipation Proclamation, enslaved people tested the omnipotence of local whites, especially in those locales where an occupying Union Army had checked white authority. In some instances, armed bands of enslaved people purportedly roamed the countryside, intimidating whites with threats.

When the war ended and the Union emerged victorious, Black men and women celebrated and confidently waited to be granted the privileges and liberties that they believed were due them both as a consequence of birthright and as a result of the loyalty they had shown during the nation's time of trial. What they received, however, fell far short of their expectations. America's commitment to the newly emancipated failed to equal their commitment to the nation.

"We have sown the wind, only to reap the whirlwind," Frederick Douglass had said in 1861. "The Republic has put one end of the chain upon the ankle of the bondman, and the other end about its own neck. The land is now to weep and howl, amid ten thousand desolations brought upon it by the sins of two centuries.... Could we write as with lightning, and speak as with the voice of thunder, we should...cry to the nation, Repent, Break Every Yoke, let the Oppressed Go Free for Herein alone is deliverance and safety!"

But the whirlwind about which Frederick Douglass spoke unleashed a new militancy that refused to be stayed. At great risk to themselves, African Americans challenged newly imposed proscriptions, sometimes boldly. In subsequent years, inspired by the activism of these Civil War–era men and women, people of color continued to press their definition of freedom and fought to ensure its enjoyment by all Americans. —*Edna Medford, Howard University*

DECEMBER 15, 16, 17 & 18, 1864. UNION (GEN. THOMAS) LOSS: 400 K, 1740 WD. CONF. (GEN. HOOD) LOSS: 287 OT F, 1524 K & W, 13,189 PRIS, 72 GUNS, WHOLE ARMY ROUTED.

BATTLE OF NASHVILLE.

CIVIL WAR BATTLES. Prior to the signing of the Emancipation Proclamation, Blacks could serve in the military as laborers but not as combatants. The perception that Blacks were docile, dependent, and therefore untrainable for battle was quickly laid to rest in 1862 when Black volunteer regiments from South Carolina waged successful raids on Confederate positions. The regiment was not authorized by the War Department and was disbanded eventually. The next year, five regiments of Black soldiers were mustered from South Carolina and inducted into the Union ranks. Despite unequal pay and substandard supplies and rations, Black soldiers fought in close to 450 battles during the Civil War, beginning in 1863 at Port Hudson and Milliken's Bend in Louisiana.

"BATTLE OF NASHVILLE," by Kurz & Allison, Chicago, 1891. Lithograph. Prints and Photographs.

THE BLACK REGIMENT,

MAY 27th, 1863.

By GEORGE H. BOKER.

Dark as the clouds of even,
Ranked in the western heaven,
Waiting the breath that lifts
All the dread mass, and drifts
Tempest and falling brand
Over a ruined land;—
So still and orderly,
Arm to arm, knee to knee,
Waiting the great event,
Stands the black regiment.

Down the long dusky line
Teeth gleam and eyeballs shine;
And the bright bayonet,
Bristling and firmly set,
Flashed with a purpose grand,
Long ere the sharp command
Of the fierce rolling drum
Told them their time had come,
Told them what work was sent
For the black regiment.

"Now," the flag-sergeant cried,
"Though death and hell beside,
Let the whole nation see
If we are fit to be
Free in this land; or bound
Down, like the whining hound—
Bound with red stripes of pain
In our old chains again!"
Oh! what a shout there went
From the black regiment!

"Charge!" Trump and drum awake,
Onward the bondmen broke;
Bayonet and sabre-stroke
Vainly opposed their rush,
Through the wild battle's crush,
With but one thought aflush,
Driving their lords like chaff,
In the guns' mouth they laugh;

Or at the slippery brands
Leaping with open hands,
Down they tear man and horse,
Down in their awful course;
Trampling with bloody heel
Over the crashing steel,
All their eyes forward bent,
Rushed the black regiment.

"Freedom!" their battle-cry—
"Freedom! or leave to die!"
Ah! and they meant the word,
Not as with us 'tis heard,
Not a mere party-shout:
They gave their spirits out;
Trusted the end to God,
And on the gory sod
Rolled in triumphant blood.
Glad to strike one free blow,
Whether for weal or woe;
Glad to breathe one free breath,
Though on the lips of death.
Praying—alas! in vain!—
That they might fall again,
So they could once more see
That burst to liberty!
This was what "freedom" lent
To the black regiment.

Hundreds on hundreds fell;
But they are resting well;
Scourges and shackles strong
Never shall do them wrong.
O, to the living few,
Soldiers, be just and true!
Hail them as comrades tried;
Fight with them side by side;
Never, in field or tent,
Scorn the black regiment!

Published by the Supervisory Committee for Recruiting Colored Regiments.

RECRUITING BLACK SOLDIERS. Black recruiters, including abolitionists Frederick Douglass, Mary Ann Shadd Cary, and Henry Highland Garnet, encouraged the recruitment of Black soldiers throughout the North. The Bureau of Colored Troops was formed by the War Department on May 22, 1863, to actively begin recruiting free Black men in the North and former slaves in the South for military service and to handle the rush of potential enlistees into all Black units.

White officers were recruited to lead the newly formed U.S. Colored Troop regiments. The first official regiment was the 54th Massachusetts Colored Regiment, which was organized in March 1863 and led by Col. Robert Gould Shaw, a white officer.

By the end of the war, 186,00 freedmen and former slaves had served in more than 170 regiments. Some 38,000 of the war's battlefield casualties were members of the U.S. Colored Troops.

COME AND JOIN US BROTHERS.
PUBLISHED BY THE SUPERVISORY COMMITTEE FOR RECRUITING COLORED REGIMENTS
1210 CHESTNUT ST. PHILADELPHIA.

"COME AND JOIN US BROTHERS," printed by P. S. Duval & Son Lithographers, Philadelphia, ca 1864. Broadside. General Museum Collection.

(OPPOSITE) **"THE BLACK REGIMENT,"** poem by George H. Boker, published by the Supervisory Committee for Recruiting Colored Regiments, 1863. Library Collection.

THE 54TH MASSACHUSETTS INFANTRY. The 54th Massachusetts Infantry was the first all-Black unit organized in the North. Most of its members were free Blacks. Lewis H. Douglass and Charles R. Douglass, sons of Frederick Douglass, were among the unit's first recruits. They came from their home of Rochester, New York, to Massachusetts in answer to the call. Lewis Douglass rose to the rank of sergeant major.

The heroic 54th is best remembered for its bravery in July 1863, as it led an unsuccessful assault on Fort Wagner, the stronghold for Charleston, South Carolina. Of its 600

men, 281 died. "Remember if I die I die in a good cause," Lewis Douglass wrote a woman friend, later his wife, two days after the battle at Fort Wagner. "I wish we had a hundred thousand colored troops—we would put an end to this war."

Sgt. William H. Carney, despite being wounded in the head, held up the American flag throughout the battle. "The old flag never touched the ground," he is quoted as saying. For his bravery, he became the first African American to receive the Medal of Honor—nearly four decades later, in 1900.

BUSINESS CARD OF SGT. MAJ. LEWIS H. DOUGLASS, 54TH MASSACHUSETTS REGIMENT, ca 1863. Frederick Douglass Collection, Howard University Museum.

BUTTON FROM THE UNIFORM OF SGT. MAJ. LEWIS H. DOUGLASS, 54TH MASSACHUSETTS REGIMENT. Brass. Frederick Douglass Collection, Howard University Museum.

(OPPOSITE) **SGT. MAJ. LEWIS H. DOUGLASS,** photographer unknown, ca 1863. Carte de visite. Frederick Douglass Papers.

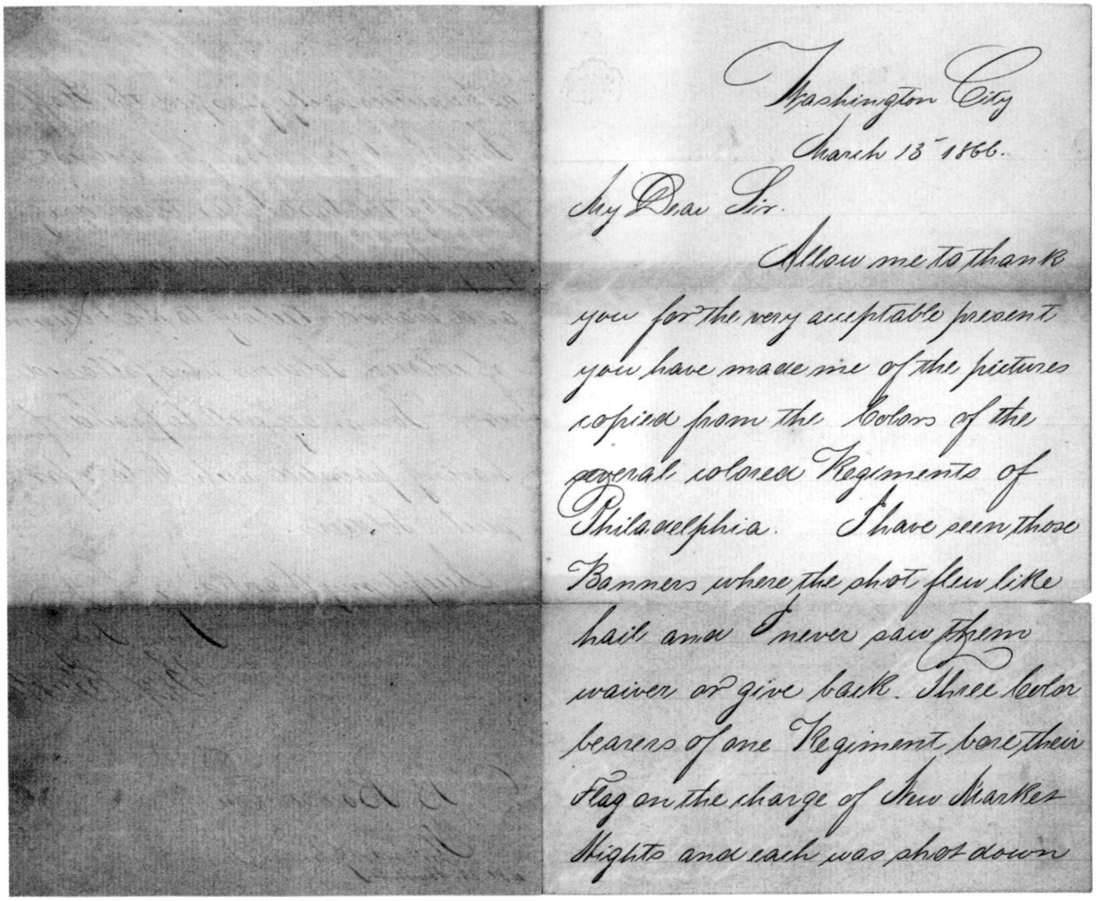

Washington City
March 13 1866.

My Dear Sir.

Allow me to thank
you for the very acceptable present
you have made me of the pictures
copied from the Colors of the
several colored Regiments of
Philadelphia. I have seen those
Banners where the shot flew like
hail and I never saw them
waiver or give back. Three Color
bearers of one Regiment bore their
Flag on the charge of New Markets
Heights and each was shot down 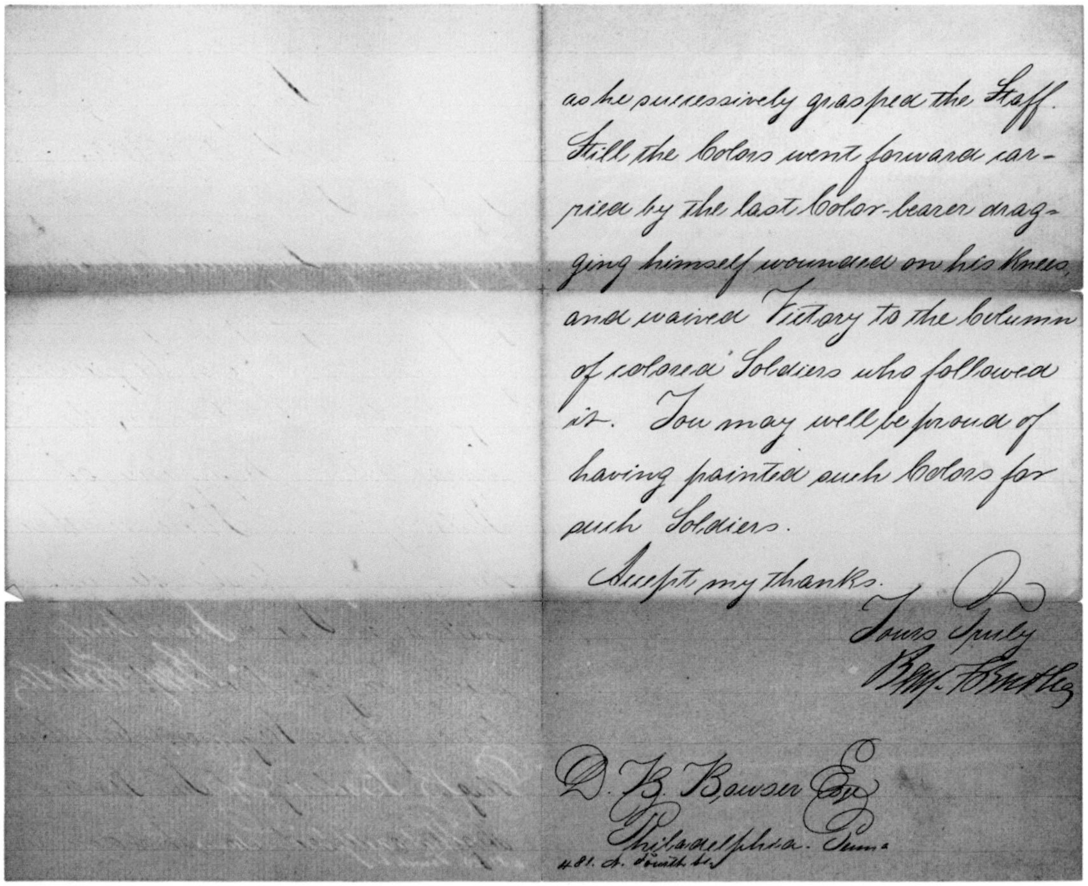
as he successively grasped the Staff.
Still the Colors went forward carried by the last Color-bearer drag-
ging himself wounded on his Knees,
and waived Victory to the Column
of colored Soldiers who followed
it. You may well be proud of
having painted such Colors for
such Soldiers.

Accept my thanks.
Yours truly
Benj. F. Butler

D. B. Bowser Esq
Philadelphia. Penna
481 S Smith St

BOWSER AND THE BANNERS. U.S. Colored Troops formed up in Pennsylvania carried regimental flags designed and produced by Philadelphia artist and photographer David Bustill Bowser. After the war, Bowser created small photographic replicas of the flags and turned them into distinctive calling cards, or cartes de visite, which he successfully sold to the returning soldiers.

The flags that Bowser designed displayed more than just information for the sake of military identification. For example, the Sixth Regiment of Philadelphia, which was known for the 1864 assault at New Market Heights, Virginia, carried a flag that stated in elegant lettering, "Freedom for All."

A logbook and letters to Bowser reveal the sentiment that Black soldiers attached to the flags, especially considering the memories they evoked of dangers experienced in battle. "Allow me to thank you for the very acceptable present you have made me of the pictures copied from the Colors of the several colored Regiments of Philadelphia," one soldier wrote him. "I have seen those Banners where the shot flew like hail and I never saw them waiver or give back."

REGIMENTAL FLAG (FRONT AND BACK) OF THE SIXTH U.S. COLORED TROOP OF PENNSYLVANIA, painted flag by David Bustill Bowser, Philadelphia, 1863. Carte de visite. Bustill-Bowser-Asbury Collection.

(OPPOSITE) **LETTER TO DAVID BUSTILL BOWSER FROM BENJAMIN BENTLEY,** March 15, 1866. Bustill-Bowser-Asbury Collection.

SOLDIERS AND SAILORS OF THE UNION

THE RISE OF THE REPUBLICAN PARTY in the mid-1850s and the election of Abraham Lincoln in 1860 gave African Americans hope that the days of slavery were numbered. Lincoln claimed no mandate to interfere with slavery in the states where it already existed, but he made clear his intention to prevent the "peculiar institution" from spreading into the West. Starting in December 1860, Lincoln presided over the secession of 11 southern states. The Confederate States of America formed in February 1861.

When the war began, Lincoln claimed that the dispute was over the Union and whether states had the constitutional right to secede. African-American leaders perceived a different kind of constitutional struggle in which the future of slavery hung in the balance. For more than a year, as Frederick Douglass and other veterans of the antislavery and antidiscrimination movement insisted that slavery was the chief bone of contention and that Black men should join the armed struggle, Lincoln and the northern electorate insisted it was a white man's war. But by the summer of 1862, Lincoln came to a new understanding: The war was about slavery, and Black men would play a part.

With varying degrees of official approval, regiments of African-American soldiers had taken shape in Kansas and in the Union-occupied portions of Louisiana and South Carolina, beginning in the summer of 1862. The Emancipation Proclamation cleared the way for large-scale enlistment of Black men, and officials in the New England states moved quickly to organize regiments, with Douglass and other prominent leaders serving as recruiters. Douglass printed the stirring call "Men of Color, To Arms!" in his monthly journal, and his two sons, Lewis and Charles, enlisted in the 54th

PAPER APPOINTING JERRY ROBINSON COMMISSARY SERGEANT, July 31, 1863. Omnium Gatherum Collection.

Massachusetts Volunteer Infantry, perhaps the most famous of the Black regiments. By war's end, nearly 200,000 men of African ancestry served in the U.S. armed forces, making up approximately 10 percent of the manpower of the Army and nearly 25 percent of the Navy's enlisted force.

The men performed well and soon captured the national imagination. In perhaps the most notable battle, the 54th Massachusetts Volunteers' assault on Fort Wagner, South Carolina, in July 1863, they removed all doubt. Popular northern newspapers began carrying illustrations depicting heroic images of Black soldiers, but just as African-American men had to struggle for the privilege to die for their country, they had to struggle to be treated as equals. Their battles against inferior pay and equipment and second-class duty assignments prompted testaments to human freedom and dignity as memorable as Lincoln's Gettysburg Address or Second Inaugural Address. Cpl. James Henry Gooding asked Lincoln: "We have done a Soldier's Duty. Why can't we have a Soldier's pay?"

Black soldiers had a greater impact on the Union's victory than numbers alone might suggest. They took special pains to free the enslaved from bondage and to spread the notion of freedom in the Confederacy. Their service helped lay the foundation of the 13th Amendment, abolishing slavery; the 14th Amendment, establishing national citizenship; and the 15th Amendment, guaranteeing universal manhood suffrage. Without their military service, the end of slavery may not have been quite as certain as it appears in retrospect, and the extension of citizenship rights to persons of African ancestry would have been delayed further. —*Joseph P. Reidy, Howard University*

"FORT PILLOW MASSACRE," by Kurz & Allison, Chicago, 1892. Color lithograph. Prints and Photographs.

WOMEN OF THE CIVIL WAR. Black women also played a significant role in the Civil War. Women were not permitted to enlist but could serve in traditional roles, such as nursing and domestic work, and in other capacities. Their personal accounts add a different perspective to descriptions of troop activities, battle scenes, and the hardships placed on Black soldiers. Harriet Tubman, who helped lead many fugitives through the Underground Railroad, served as a scout, a nurse, and a spy for the Union Army. She encouraged slaves to escape and serve in the Army and led several raids herself. Some women had the opportunity to learn to read or write before the Civil War and contributed by reading and writing letters for soldiers. Educator Charlotte Forten Grimké taught for two years on

PINCUSHION BELONGING TO ELIZABETH KECKLEY, 1895. Cook Family Papers.

CHARLOTTE FORTEN GRIMKÉ, photograph by Estabrook, ca 1860. Carte de visite. Archibald Grimké Papers.

the South Carolina Sea Islands after Union forces secured the area. She related her experience in *Life on the Sea Islands,* published in the May and June 1864 issues of the *Atlantic Monthly.* Her essays gave an early firsthand account of the impact of emancipation on newly freed slaves. In her personal account, nurse Susie King Taylor describes many gruesome battle scenes and the valor of the Black soldiers she served with. She and her husband taught soldiers to read and write. Elizabeth Keckley, a former slave, secured her freedom and fled to Washington, D.C., in 1861 and established herself as a dressmaker. One of her clients was President Abraham Lincoln's wife. Keckley sympathized with other former slaves and started the Contraband Relief Association.

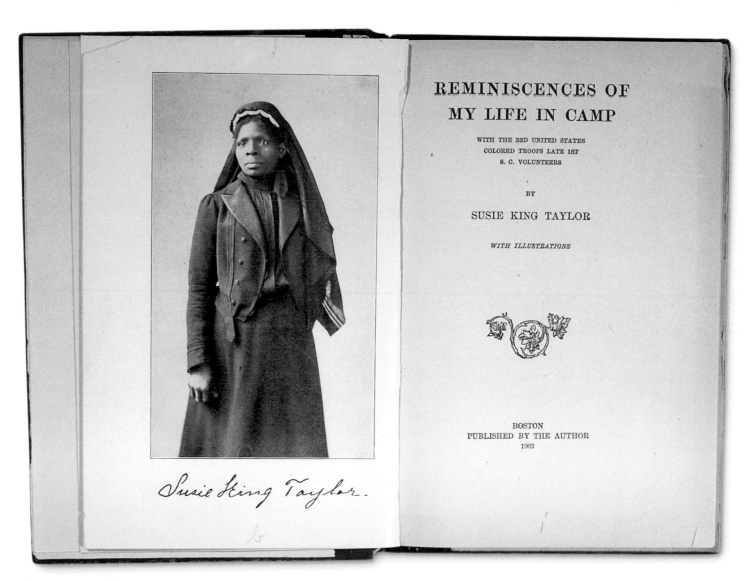

REMINISCENCES OF MY LIFE IN CAMP WITH THE 33D UNITED STATES COLORED TROOPS LATE 1ST S.C. VOLUNTEERS, by Susie King Taylor, Boston, 1902. Library Collection.

CHAPTER 7
Post-Civil War
1865-1878

This is the time when every thinking man must come forward and give his views to the People, it is the time they most need talking to, in order that they may be educated up to the requirements of the times. The customs and habits contracted during 240-odd years of slavery and oppression can not pass away in a day. Nor will it ever pass away unless we seek that information which will qualify us for a higher station. No nation ever has, or ever can, obtain the respect and confidence of the other nations of the earth until it has made some effort in its own behalf.

Pinckney Benton Stewart Pinchback,
1865 or 1866 Speech, Montgomery, Alabama

1865-1878 *Reconstruction was a time of radical change that continued to divide the U.S. over race issues. The reunited government introduced several programs to address the needs of newly freed slaves while rebuilding a political and economic infrastructure no longer sustained by forced labor. Black officials, some former slaves, were appointed to political offices at the state and local level for the first time. The Bureau of Refugees, Freedmen, and Abandoned Lands was established on March 3, 1865, to assist former slaves in adjusting to life as freedmen. Gen. Oliver Otis Howard, the bureau's first commissioner, later became president of the university now remembered by his name—Howard.*

Reconstruction was also a time of readjustment, as illustrated in the records and printed material that have survived. Mustering-out papers and pension records provide some insight into the status of Black soldiers returning home, while photographs provide a visual record of personal and professional accomplishments. Personal letters and the announcements and programs generated by benevolent and literary societies reflect the desire to uplift from within the race in the quest to be recognized as full American citizens.

THE QUEST FOR FREEDOM AND RECONCILIATION

IN HIS SECOND INAUGURAL ADDRESS, on March 4, 1865, Abraham Lincoln suggested that the Civil War might be perceived as God's punishment of the nation for having kept human beings in bondage. "If God wills that [the war] continue until all the wealth piled by the bondsman's 250 years of unrequited toil shall be sunk, and until every drop of blood drawn with the lash shall be paid by another drawn with the sword, as was said 3,000 years ago," he asserted, "so still it must be said, 'The judgments of the Lord are true and righteous altogether.' " Concluding his address with a call to complete the parallel missions of abolishing slavery and "bind[ing] up the nation's wounds," Lincoln provided a conceptual paradigm and implied an organic link between Black freedom and national reconciliation.

Reconstruction plans prescribed by Lincoln in 1863 and Andrew Johnson in 1865 greatly differed from the congressional plan of 1867. Presidential reconstruction provided relief from "unrequited toil" and "the lash" but allowed white Southerners to be the sole determinants of any further definitions of Black freedom. Despite Lincoln's and Johnson's suggestions, Black Southerners were not allowed to participate in the process. White Southerners elected former Confederate leaders to high state and national offices. Their state and local governments enacted codes that kept Black freedmen a servile workforce. Individuals and organizations like the Ku Klux Klan violently attempted to force the freedmen to continue to observe the etiquette of slavery.

UNKNOWN WOMAN, photographer unknown, ca 1870. Hand-colored tintype. Letitia Young Woodson Collection.

"Emancipation is one fact, effective liberty is another," declared the *New Orleans Tribune*, a Black newspaper, in January 1865. Even before the war was over, freedmen were asserting the right to own land, to be paid for their labor, to move about from place to place, to be secure in their persons, to exercise political rights, to enjoy equal protection under the law, and to establish autonomous social institutions such as stable families, churches, and schools. Moderate white Republicans in the North began to embrace the more expansive ideals of what Black freedom should entail.

Congressional Republicans wrested control of Reconstruction from the executive branch of government. In 1866 Congress passed in rapid succession the Civil Rights Bill, the proposed 14th Amendment, and a second Freedmen's Bureau Bill. In the Reconstruction Act—passed over Johnson's veto in March 1867 and supplemented by later legislation—Congress stipulated that seceded states could resume their place in the Union only if they provided for manhood suffrage and ratified the 14th Amendment, giving Blacks national and state citizenship and federal protection of their rights to due process. States risked reduced representation in Congress if they denied the vote to adult male citizens for reasons other than "participation in rebellion, or other crime."

By the end of 1870, the 13th and 14th Amendments to the Constitution had been joined by the 15th Amendment, prohibiting states from denying citizens the right to vote "on account of race, color, or previous condition of servitude." Congress then enacted the Civil Rights Act of 1875, prohibiting racial discrimination in places of public accommodation and on public conveyances.

As a result of the freedmen's enfranchisement, the 16-year-old Republican Party had become a national political party. Fourteen Blacks served in the U.S. House of Representatives, and Hiram Revels and Blanche K. Bruce represented Mississippi in the U.S. Senate. More than 600 Blacks sat in southern state legislatures but composed a majority only in South Carolina. They also served in the executive and judicial branches of several state governments and in a variety of local offices. Some were carpetbaggers, others freeborn residents of the antebellum South who had been educated in the North. Still others were freedmen, some of whom had become literate as a result of the efforts of the Union Army, teachers from the North, and the Freedmen's Bureau.

Southern Republicans helped establish public schools, for whites as well as Blacks. They established hospitals, insane asylums, and orphanages, and they made provisions for poor relief. In the area of civil rights, they passed state suffrage laws, repealed or modified Black codes, reformed their judicial and penal systems, and expanded some rights for women. Several states in the Deep South passed laws prohibiting discrimination in public places and vehicles. Only New Orleans and the state of South Carolina, however, provided for integrated schools.

Neither the Radicals in Congress nor the Republican state governments effectively addressed the former slaves' desire for land, but some freedmen were able to purchase confiscated, abandoned, or unutilized land. In 1890 Black Southerners owned about eight million acres. In Virginia in 1900, about 60 percent of Black farmers owned their own land. For a majority of freedmen, however, land ownership proved to be an elusive quest. A majority of those who farmed became laborers or tenants. By

1900 more than half of the tenants were sharecroppers who, when trapped in the crop lien system, worked under conditions reminiscent of slavery.

White terrorism by the Ku Klux Klan, founded in Tennessee in 1866, and similar organizations was characteristic of white southern opposition to Radical Reconstruction. Through numerous violent means, white terrorists sought to drive Blacks and their white allies from the political arena and to reestablish white supremacy. Blacks often fought back, pitching battles between white terrorists and state and local militias reminiscent of the Civil War. Congress passed the Enforcement Acts of the early 1870s. The Klan was suppressed, but other groups continued a campaign of violence for years.

BETWEEN 1870 AND 1875 Democrats returned to power in seven of the restored states. Their 1877 return to power in the last three Republican-controlled states—Florida, Louisiana, and South Carolina—was marked by high political drama. In the presidential election of 1876, disputed electoral votes from those states were awarded to Rutherford B. Hayes, the Republican candidate. He won by one vote. As President, Hayes ordered the federal troops who had protected the Republicans in those states back to their barracks. Radical Reconstruction was over.

By the end of 1877 the political structure of the nation had been mended, but the definition of Black freedom as effective liberty was threatened. In 1883 the Supreme Court invalidated the Civil Rights Act of 1875 on the grounds that the 14th Amendment did not prohibit discriminatory actions by private parties. In 1896, in *Plessey v. Ferguson*, the Supreme Court upheld discriminatory acts by states, confirming the legality of separate but equal provisions for Black and white citizens. In 1867 more than 104,000 Black Alabamians were registered to vote, by 1900 only 3,000 were.

The end of political Reconstruction did not end social reconstruction, though. Of their own accord and with the assistance of the Freedmen's Bureau, Black Southerners removed the shackles of slavery from their family lives. Some family members, separated by slavery, reunited. They reaffirmed old bonds and established new bonds through wedding ceremonies and marriage licenses. They resisted the efforts of white planters to use their children as laborers. And some of their wives initially refused to work in the fields of white landowners.

The Black church also reinforced the Black family. Former slaves separated from white churches or held their own worship services, free from white surveillance. The number of Black churches of various denominations increased dramatically throughout the postwar South. Beyond their religious functions, they served as morale boosters, preservers of expressive culture, providers of social welfare, and laboratories of leadership. Before public education became available to Black children, individual churches established elementary schools. Some religious denominations started and maintained secondary schools and colleges. Black and white Northerners came south as teachers, and white philanthropists helped to finance Black colleges. The institutions of family, church, and school thus survived the overthrow of political Reconstruction and remained the pillars of stability and fountains of vitality for Black communities during the era of racial apartheid that followed.
—*Arnold H. Taylor, professor emeritus, Howard University*

T'n Hall, Waterville.
WEDNESDAY EV'G, NOV. 8.

SHEPPARD'S JUBILEE SINGERS
A GENUINE SLAVE BAND, IN
JUBILEE SONGS

They are genuine Colored People, under the Leadership of ANDREW SHEPPARD, Thirty years a Slave, formerly the property of Gen. Robert E. Lee, at Arlington, Va., emancipated by Abraham Lincoln's Great Proclamation of Freedom. These Singers make no pretentions to musical abilities, theybeing unable to read or write. All having been Slaves they give the truest and best representation of Slave Life on the Old Plantation.

SOLEMN, SACRED SONGS OF THE OLD PLANTATION,

WHICH FOR MELODY AND HARMONY ARE UNSURPASSED.

Organized by Rev. Father Hawley, City Missionary, in the City of Hartford, Ct., for over 20 years.

From the HARTFORD COURANT, Feb. 17th, 1875.

We have taken pains to investigate the claims of the company, and from what we can learn, judge that their singing is marked by the same solemn earnestness and true feeling which so distinguished the original company. They make no pretensions to being other than what they really are—a company giving concerts for the sake of procuring means for the maintainance of their old people, and the education of themselves and their children. The names shown us attached to their recommendations are those of persons in whom we have the utmost confidence.

PRICES .... **15, 25 & 35 CENTS.**

DOORS OPEN AT 7 O'CLOCK.   CONCERT TO COMMENCE AT 8 O'CLOCK.   (Franklin Print, Providence, R. I.)

JUBILEE. Most jubilee singing groups were formed in the years immediately following the Civil War. Made up of former slaves, these groups performed a repertoire that ranged from sacred songs sung on plantations to operatic pieces by European composers. The most popular group was the Fisk Jubilee Singers, organized in 1867 by George L. White at Fisk University in Nashville, Tennessee. The original group consisted of nine students who performed locally and traveled throughout the North, offering concerts to raise money for the school. In several years' time, they were touring Europe. Their efforts brought enough money back to the school to build Jubilee Hall, a Victorian building still standing today, which houses a larger-than-life mural of the original Fisk Jubilee Singers commissioned by Queen Victoria. The Fisk Jubilee Singers still perform today. "We stand on the shoulders of the original Jubilee Singers," the group proudly claims today, "continuing their legacy, as we sing Negro spirituals."

(OPPOSITE) SHEPPARD'S JUBILEE SINGERS, ca 1880. Broadside. Omnium Gatherum Collection.

TRAVEL LOG OF THE FISK JUBILEE SINGERS, 1880s. Log entry kept by Maggie Wilson Smoot. Omnium Gatherum Collection.

FISK JUBILEE SINGERS, photograph by Allen and Howell, ca 1890. Prints and Photographs.

GEO. E. BARRETT.   JENNIE JACKSON.   F. J. LOUDIN.   R. A. HALL.
MAGGIE PORTER.   ELLA SHEPPARD.   MABEL LEWIS.   PATTI MALONE.

HOWARD UNIVERSITY, 1867-1910

THE STORY OF HOWARD UNIVERSITY has been described as "one of the great romances of American education." It is a story of extraordinary men and women accomplishing noble deeds, of institutional survival wrought by biracial cooperation, of social and governmental largesse, and of interaction among peoples of different racial, sexual, economic, and cultural backgrounds.

Established by an act of Congress in May 1867, Howard traces its genesis to a November 1866 meeting of the First Congregational Society of Washington, D.C. Concerned with the plight of African Americans—4,000,000 newly emancipated and 250,000 born free—by January 1867, society members shifted their vision from a theological seminary to a university. The first board of trustees adopted a policy ensuring that the university would remain open to all individuals, irrespective of race, sex, creed, or national origin. They saw it as a bold, new experiment of cosmopolitan dimensions.

The first challenge was the establishment of an educational vehicle that African Americans supported. From 1867 to 1910 educated African Americans served on the faculty and staff, held high administrative posts, and made up a significant fraction of the student body. The second challenge was the formation of biracial allegiance, to sustain the school's further development. From 1865 to 1910, males and females, old and young, single and married, white and Black, native and foreign—individuals of literate, semiliterate, and illiterate capacities—engaged in the Howard experience.

The third challenge was sustaining a university financially in a hostile environment. From 1867 to 1873, Gen. Oliver Otis Howard, the third university president and the commissioner of the Freedmen's Bureau, provided federal funds and services-in-kind from the bureau. Losing federal assistance in 1873, the university struggled to maintain itself with private donations. From 1879 to 1910, the university received "congressional financial gifts" totaling $1,217,848. These gifts, and future federal appropriations, generated a symbiotic relationship between Howard and the federal government.

The final challenge was the establishment of a multiracial, coeducational university community. The university's first four students in 1867 were Caucasian females. The international student body included individuals from more than 20 countries—from Barbados to China, Cuba to India, Jamaica to Korea, South Africa to Turkey. No other American university could boast such diversity.
—*Clifford L. Muse, Jr., Howard University*

ACT OF INCORPORATION, HOWARD UNIVERSITY, 1867. Howard University Collection, Howard University Museum.

(OPPOSITE) **LAND DEED, JOHN A. SMITH TO HOWARD UNIVERSITY,** 1867. Howard University Archives.

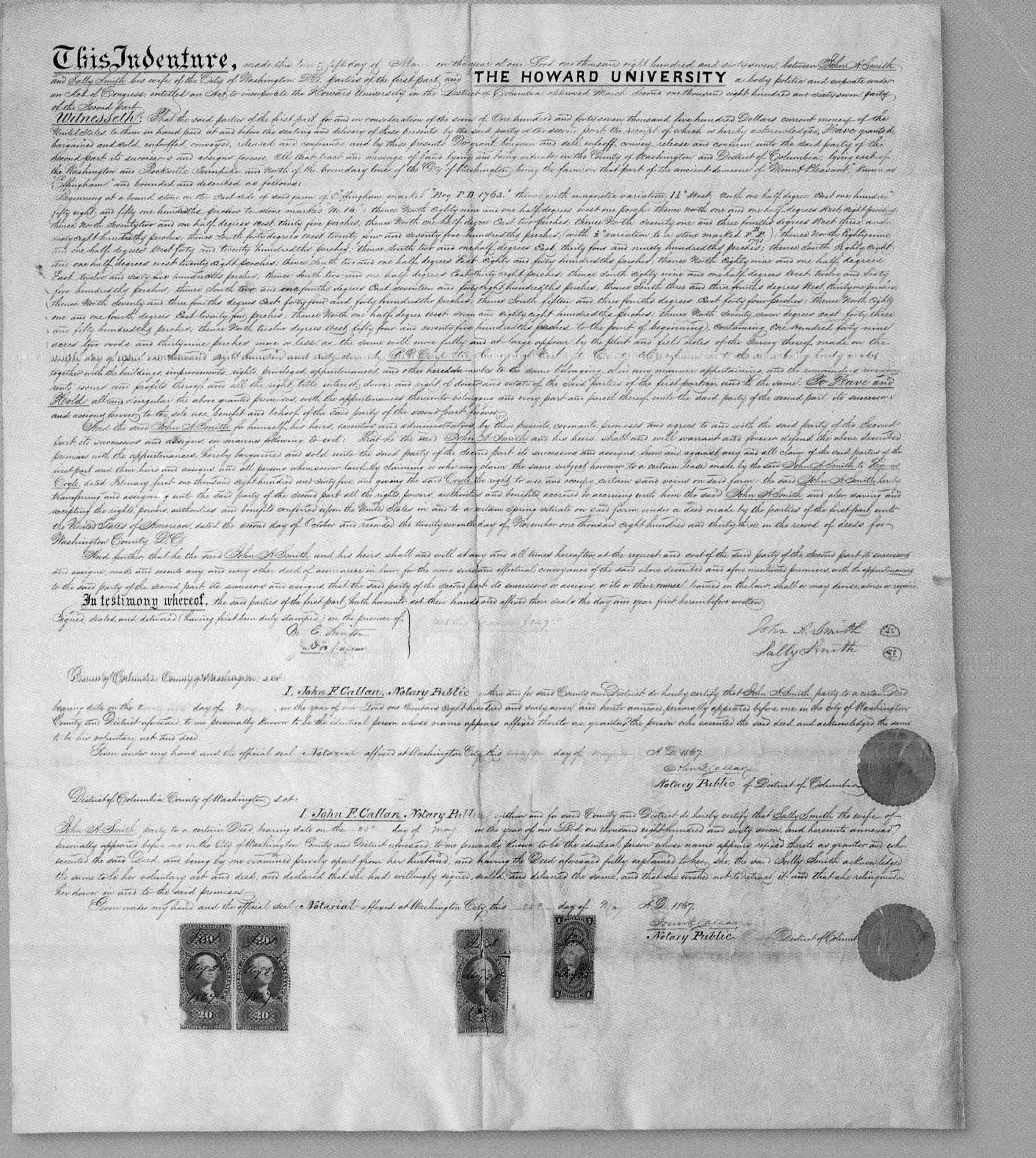

This Indenture, made this twenty fifth day of May in the year of our Lord one thousand eight hundred and sixty seven, between John A. Smith and Sally Smith his wife of the City of Washington D.C. parties of the first part, and **THE HOWARD UNIVERSITY** a body politic and corporate under an Act of Congress entitled an Act to incorporate the Howard University in the District of Columbia approved March Second one thousand eight hundred and sixty seven party of the Second part

Witnesseth: That the said parties of the first part for and in consideration of the sum of One hundred and forty seven thousand, five hundred Dollars current money of the United States, to them in hand paid, at and before the sealing and delivery of these presents, by the said party of the second part, the receipt of which is hereby acknowledged, Have granted, bargained and sold, enfeoffed, conveyed, released and confirmed and by these presents Do grant, bargain and sell, enfeoff, convey, release and confirm, unto the said party of the Second part its successors and assigns forever, All that tract and message of land lying and being situate in the County of Washington and District of Columbia, lying east of the Washington and Rockville Turnpike and North of the boundary line of the City of Washington being the farm or that part of the ancient demesne of "Mount Pleasant," known as "Effingham," and bounded and described as follows:

Beginning at a bound stone on the East side of said farm of Effingham marked "Beg P.D. 1763," thence with magnetic variation 1½° West, North one half degree East one hundred fifty eight and fifty one hundredths perches to stone marked No. 16; thence North eighty nine and one half degrees west one perch; thence North one and one half degrees West, eight perches; thence North Seventy two and one half degrees West, thirty five perches; thence North one half degree East two perches; thence North seventy one and three fourths degrees West three and sixty eight hundredths perches; thence South forty degrees west twenty four and seventy five hundredths perches, (with ½° variation to a stone marked P.B.P. 1791); thence North Eighty nine and one half degrees West forty and twenty hundredths perches; thence South two and one half degrees East, thirty four and ninety hundredths perches; thence South Eighty eight and one half degrees west twenty eight perches; thence South two and one half degrees East eighty and forty hundredths perches; thence North eighty nine and one half degrees East twelve and sixty five hundredths perches; thence South two and one half degrees East thirty eight perches; thence South eighty nine and one half degrees West, twelve and sixty five hundredths perches; thence South two and one fourth degrees East seventeen and forty eight hundredths perches; thence South three and three fourths degrees West, thirty one perches; thence North Seventy and three fourths degrees East forty four and forty hundredths perches; thence South fifteen and three fourths degrees East forty four perches; thence North Eighty one and one fourth degrees East twenty four perches; thence North one half degree West seven and eighty eight hundredths perches; thence North Seventy seven degrees East forty three and fifty hundredths perches; thence North twelve degrees West fifty four and seventy five hundredths perches to the point of beginning, containing One Hundred forty nine acres two roods and thirty nine perches more or less, as the same will more fully and at large appear by the plat and field notes of the Survey thereof made on the [illegible] R. R. [illegible]

together with the buildings, improvements, rights, privileges, appurtenances, and other hereditaments to the same belonging, or in any manner appertaining, and the remainders, reversions, rents issues and profits thereof and all the right, title, interest, dower and right of dower and estate of the said parties of the first part in and to the same. **To Have and Hold** all and singular the above granted premises, with the appurtenances thereunto belonging and every part and parcel thereof, unto the said party of the second part, its successors and assigns forever, to the sole use, benefit and behoof of the said party of the second part forever.

And the said John A. Smith for himself, his heirs, executors and administrators, by these presents, covenants, promises and agrees to and with the said party of the Second part, its successors and assigns, in manner following, to wit: That he the said John A. Smith and his heirs shall and will warrant and forever defend the above described premises with the appurtenances, hereby bargained and sold unto the said party of the Second part its successors and assigns, from and against any and all claim of the said parties of the first part and their heirs and assigns, and all persons whomsoever lawfully claiming, or who may claim the same subject however to a certain lease made by the said John A. Smith to Thomas Coyle, dated February first one thousand eight hundred and sixty five, and giving the said Coyle the right to use and occupy certain sand veins on said farm: the said John A. Smith hereby transferring and assigning unto the said party of the second part all the rights, powers, authorities and benefits accrued or accruing unto him the said John A. Smith, and also saving and excepting the rights, powers, authorities and benefits conferred upon the United States in and to a certain Spring situate on said farm, under a deed made by the parties of the first part, unto the United States of America, dated the second day of October and recorded the twenty seventh day of November one thousand eight hundred and thirty three, in the record of deeds for Washington County, D.C.

And further, that he the said John A. Smith and his heirs, shall and will at any and all times hereafter, at the request and cost of the said party of the Second part its successors and assigns, make and execute any and every other deed of assurance in law, for the more sure and effectual conveyance of the said above described and afore mentioned premises, with the appurtenances to the said party of the second part, its successors and assigns, that the said party of the second part its successors or assigns, or its or their counsel learned in the law, shall or may devise, advise or require.

In testimony whereof, the said parties of the first part, hath hereunto set their hands and affixed their seals the day and year first hereinbefore written.

Signed, sealed, and delivered (having first been duly stamped) in the presence of
W. C. Smith
[illegible]

John A. Smith (Seal)
Sally Smith (Seal)

District of Columbia County of Washington, Sct.

I, John F. Callan, Notary Public within and for said County and District do hereby certify that John A. Smith party to a certain Deed, bearing date on the twenty fifth day of May, in the year of our Lord one thousand eight hundred and sixty seven, and hereto annexed, personally appeared before me in the city of Washington County and District aforesaid, to me personally known to be the identical person whose name appears affixed thereto as grantor, the person who executed the said deed, and acknowledged the same to be his voluntary act and deed.

Given under my hand and the official seal Notarial affixed at Washington City this twenty fifth day of May A.D. 1867.

John F. Callan
Notary Public of District of Columbia

District of Columbia County of Washington, Sct:

I, John F. Callan, Notary Public within and for said County and District do hereby certify that Sally Smith the wife of John A. Smith, party to a certain Deed, bearing date on the 25th day of May in the year of our Lord one thousand eight hundred and sixty seven, and hereunto annexed, personally appeared before me in the City of Washington County and District aforesaid, to me personally known to be the identical person whose name appears affixed thereto as grantor and who executed the said Deed, and being by me examined privily apart from her husband, and having the Deed aforesaid fully explained to her, she, the said Sally Smith acknowledged the same to be her voluntary act and deed, and declared that she had willingly signed, sealed, and delivered the same, and that she wishes not to retract it, and that she relinquishes her dower in and to the said premises.

Given under my hand and the official seal Notarial affixed at Washington City this 25th day of May A.D. 1867.

John F. Callan
Notary Public District of Columbia

STUDENTS IN FRONT OF HOWARD HALL, photograph by J. W. & J. S. Moulton, 1870. Stereograph. Howard University Archives.

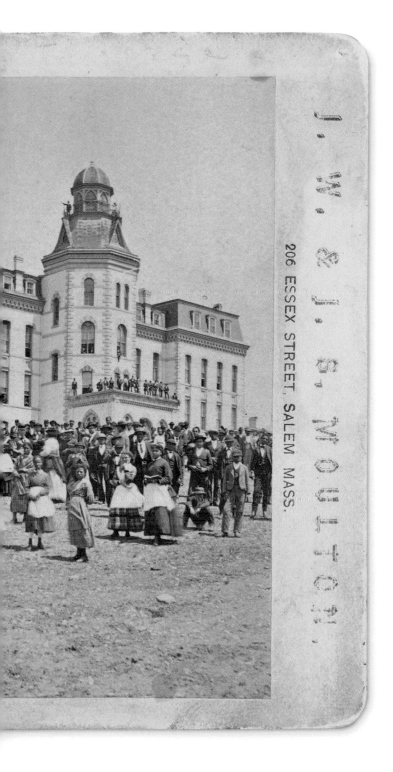

J. W. & J. S. MOULTON
206 ESSEX STREET, SALEM, MASS.

AN INTEGRATED UNIVERSITY.

Founded just two years after the end of the Civil War, Howard University was conceived as a democratic university, open to all men and women of all races. As such, it was the only integrated university of its time in the United States. The original university seal depicted members of different races and carried the motto "Equal rights and knowledge for all." Howard was the third university to be founded in the District of Columbia, the nation's capital. Georgetown University was established in 1789, George Washington University in 1821. Howard opened by offering a liberal arts program of study according to a mission that echoed that of the Freedmen's Bureau: to promote the welfare of freedmen.

Oliver Otis Howard, an abolitionist before the Civil War, advanced to the rank of major general during the war and fought valiantly in many battles, including Bull Run and Gettysburg. After the war, he ran the Freedmen's Bureau and was superintendent of West Point. He helped found the university that was named for him.

CORPORATE SEAL, HOWARD UNIVERSITY, 1867-1910.
Howard University Archives.

BLACK AMERICANS ENTER POLITICS. Beginning in 1867, Congress passed Reconstruction Acts that granted Black males who had been slaves the right to vote and the right to hold public office.

In 1868, John W. Manard was elected to the House of Representatives from Louisiana but was barred by white members of Congress from assuming his seat. He asserted his right to plead his case before Congress and became the first Black to speak from the House floor.

Joseph Hayne Rainey was the first elected Black seated in the U.S. House of Representatives. Born to slave parents in Georgetown, South Carolina, and by trade a barber, Rainey was elected to Congress in 1870 and reelected for four more consecutive terms.

Hiram Revels, representing Mississippi in the U.S. Senate in 1870, was the nation's first Black senator. A minister in the A.M.E. Church in Baltimore, he served in the Union Army and fought at the Battle of Vicksburg. The Mississippi Legislature appointed him to the Senate, where he served one year and spoke out against racial injustice.

"THE FIRST COLORED SENATOR AND REPRESENTATIVES, IN THE 41ST AND 42ND CONGRESS OF THE UNITED STATES," Currier & Ives, New York, 1872. Black and white lithograph. Prints and Photographs.

(OPPOSITE) **DESK BELONGING TO CONGRESSMAN JOSEPH HAYNE RAINEY,** used 1870-79. General Museum Collection.

"THE CAKE WALK: BESTOWING THE FAVOR," photographer unknown, ca 1890. Stereograph.
Prints and Photographs.

The Cake Walk: Bestowing the Favor.

TAKING THE CAKE IN THE EARLY JIM CROW ERA. The cakewalk was a competition dance that originated on plantations as an exaggerated rendition of European parlor dances. Its name comes from the rewards, slices of cake, given to the best dancers. In plantation days, slave owners watched the cakewalk for entertainment. After emancipation, the dance became an even more elaborate spectacle, appreciated by white and Black alike, and considered the first and most popular social dance that combined African, European, and American traditions. Music from the cakewalk tradition influenced ragtime and turn-of-the-century composers in both America and Europe, including John Philip Sousa and Claude Debussy.

This portrayal of a cakewalk is printed on a stereograph card, an amusement technology of the late 19th century. When seen through a special viewer, the card conveyed a three-dimensional image, like film-based View-Masters of the mid-20th century. Stereography was the dominant form of photography in the late 19th century, the Internet of its day in that it educated the average person about art, culture, customs, geography, and ethnography. Sometimes stereograph representations confirmed racial stereotypes, as in this image—for these are white dancers dressed in blackface, mirroring the original Black cakewalk for white onlookers.

CHAPTER 8

Life and War Under Jim Crow

1890-1945

The eagle is universally regarded as a noble bird. He comes down to us through history and heraldry as emblematic of dignity, strength, and courage. The Roman Eagle typified the glory and grandeur of that far-flung and far-famed empire. The eagle has been adopted as the symbol of the land of the free and the home of the brave and is stamped, in bas-relief, upon our most sacred emblem—The Almighty Dollar. On the other hand, Jim-Crow is a spurious bird and finds a place in the fowl family only by the most curious coincidence of name and color. As the term has taken character from association and use, its imputed qualities and characteristics are most clearly those of the American buzzard, whose name suggests obliquity and scorn.

Kelly Miller, 1919
Speech, "The National Bird: Eagle or Jim Crow?"

1890-1945   *After the end of Reconstruction, racism, in the form of Jim Crow, further divided Americans. After the removal of Federal troops in the South, Blacks were now exposed to further injustices, violence, and restrictions, sparking their desire to improve opportunities and inspiring a concerted effort to force change.*

Between the end of Reconstruction and World War II, Black Americans moved within the U.S. in three major waves. In 1879 some 6,000 citizens embarked on a rural-to-rural migration, searching for better farmland. Until the end of the First World War, Blacks increasingly moved to industrial cities in the South, like Atlanta and Birmingham. During and after World War I, more than 700,000 migrated to urban centers in the North, like New York, Chicago, and Detroit, stirring the exploration of a Black consciousness in the arts as well as in social, political, and civic activities.

Although many opportunities were denied to people of color, Blacks contributed fully in the fight for democracy at home and abroad. They acted through newly formed fraternal, self-help, and civic organizations like the NAACP and the Alpha Kappa Alpha Sorority, Inc., both founded in the first decade of the 20th century.

THE AMERICAN NEGRO MILITARY EXPERIENCE

THE TRADITION OF NEGRO MEN IN AMERICAN MILITARY SERVICE UNITS began almost as soon as the American colonies were established. Records collected under the direction of the Chief of Colored Troops Division, Adjutant General's Office, show that as early as 1639, colored men gravitated to the armed services in order to attain the rights and fulfill the obligations of citizenship.

Negroes numbered among the colonial militia in 1754, when George Washington rescued Colonial and British troops from Fort Duquesne during the French and Indian War. They were among the first to die for liberty and freedom in the Boston Massacre in 1775. Organized into a Battalion of Free Men of Color, their distinguished actions helped Gen. Andrew Jackson save the day at New Orleans during the War of 1812. There can be no doubt that the 38,000 U.S. Colored Troops who lost their lives during the Civil War contributed heavily to the victory of the Union forces. Negro contingents were also at San Juan Hill during the Spanish-American War with the Rough Riders.

Seven years after the end of World War I, in October 1925, when the War Department sought to determine the use of Negro manpower in future mobilization efforts, Maj. Gen. H. E. Ely, commandant of the Army's War College, in a memorandum for the chief of staff, ignored the Negro soldiers' successful combat exploits under the administration of French military officers, and instead

"WE ARE AMERICANS TOO," by Andy Razaf, Eubie Blake, and Charles L. Cooke, 1941. Arthur B. Spingarn Sheet Music Collection.

considered solely their limited combat role and overriding involvement with menial tasks under American officers. The memo cited the following factors in its conclusion: "Because of their smaller cranial capacity, the American Negro has not progressed as other subspecies of the human family. As a race the Negro has not developed leadership qualities. His mental inferiority, inherent weakness of character, his subservience, his belief in his own inferiority to white soldiers, his susceptibility to the influence of crowd psychology and the fact that he cannot control himself in the fear of danger as a white man can, should be used as a guide in the revision of the War Department General Mobilization Plan, and political or racial pressure should not be allowed to alter it." These attitudes and practices were in operation in the American military and in society as a whole in 1941 and were the determinants of Negroes' military existence when they first began to qualify as pilots with the U.S. Air Corps.

DURING THE 1940s, when the Negro vote became crucial to Franklin Roosevelt's third election campaign, against Wendell Wilkie; when the threat of a march on Washington appeared imminent; and when Negro resistance to the draft became a looming possibility, the President was prodded into broadening opportunities for Negro soldiers in the armed forces, and Negro civilians in defense industries. The most encouraging result of this community agitation came in 1941 with the activation by the U.S. Army Air Corps of the 99th Pursuit Squadron and the acceptance of Negro cadets for training as military pilots. Subsequent graduates from this program became known popularly as the Tuskegee Airmen, since the Tuskegee Army Air Field (TAAF) was the only training facility at which military flight training for Negroes could be obtained.

The training of flying cadets, who would become the first all-Negro 99th Pursuit Squadron at Tuskegee, Alabama, was looked upon as an experiment by the military establishment and by many in the white civil community as well, who had never seen Negroes fly airplanes. The few who had, possibly thought them to be exceptional individuals but questioned their ability to fly under the discipline of combat or to match wits with the enemy.

In the Negro community, however, there was never such a notion of military flying as being an experimental process. Segments of the Negro community had been air-minded since Charles Lindbergh flew the Atlantic. As early as 1931, a Negro application for pilot training was received and rejected by the Air Corps. Lt. Benjamin O. Davis, Jr., who was well qualified for assignment to pilot training upon graduation from West Point Military Academy in 1936, was denied the opportunity because of his race. At the same time, Federal Aviation Administration records for January 1939 list 125 Negro civilians who held various commercial, limited, private, and student pilot licenses. The passage of Public Law 18, admitting Negro men to federally funded Civilian Pilot Training Programs, further expanded Negro participation in aviation pursuits and deepened their enthusiasm and dreams of flying. For the Negro community, military pilot training was merely a demonstration of the ability of Negroes to measure arms with any race, particularly white Americans, when given equal opportunity.

George Leland Washington, who is often considered the father of Negro aviation in America and was director of pilot training programs at Tuskegee, believed that their individual performances in civil aviation had proved the ability of Negroes to fly, and likewise, that civil aviation represented a primary prerequisite for success in military aviation. For the Negro community, it was just another demonstration of will and determination.

The activation of the 99th Pursuit Squadron occurred in March 1941, at Chanute Field, Rantoul, Illinois, where 5 aviation cadets and 271 enlisted men learned their technical skills. The Flying School was activated in July 1941, at the Tuskegee Army Air Field when the first 13 pilot trainees were accepted into Class 42-C. Seven months later, on March 6, 1942, Captain Davis and four flying cadets became the first Negro military pilots ever to receive their wings and commissions in the U.S. Army Air Corps.

Subsequently, 67 flight training classes would graduate and commission 992 fighter and bomber pilots before the program was discontinued at Tuskegee Army Air Field in February 1946. Roughly half of these would participate in aerial combat over the North Africa-Mediterranean-European theaters of war and would go on to earn two Presidential Unit Citations for their combat accomplishments.

The remaining pilots, who did not see combat overseas, nevertheless distinguished themselves in the American theater, where many, as members of the 477th Bombardment Group (Medium) (Colored), and at the risk of their lives and careers, refused to obey direct, albeit illegal, orders issued by superior officers that would have demeaned their character, dignity, and stature as officers in the U.S. Air Force.

In 1945 at Freeman Field Army Air Force base near Seymour, Indiana, members of the 477th attempted to integrate an all-white officers' club. The so-called Freeman Field Mutiny resulted in the arrests of 162 Black officers, the court-martialing of 3, and the conviction of 1. Despite the efforts of the air bases's PR office to justify the exclusionary policy, the resulting outcry led to public scrutiny. The officers were eventually vindicated, and the incident was seen as a watershed in attempts to integrate the armed forces as well as segregated public facilities.

FINALLY, BUT ALSO IMPORTANT, these Negro flying units were activated to achieve the mission of taking war to America's enemies. The flying echelon, as previously noted, consisted of 996 single- and twin-engine–trained pilots assigned variously to the 99th Pursuit (later Fighter) Squadron, 332nd Fighter Group, and 477th Bombardment Group. But relatively little is known about the estimated 18,000 officers and predominantly enlisted personnel who made up the 34 numbered Air Force and administrative, technical ground support, and service units. These personnel provided all necessary support for America's segregated, all-Negro Air Force during World War II, and afterward through July 1948, when President Harry S. Truman issued Executive Order 9981, effectively bringing about the deactivation of exclusively Negro units in the American military.
—*William F. Holton, National Historian, Tuskegee Airmen, Inc.*

CHARGE OF THE 24TH AND 25TH COLORED INFANTRY AND RESCUE OF ROUGH RIDERS AT SAN JUAN HILL, JULY 2nd, 1898.

THE BATTLE OF SAN JUAN HILL. African-

American soldiers who had fought in the Civil War could continue their military service by joining either the 9th or 10th Cavalries or the 24th or 25th Infantries. Every one of these was a peacekeeping unit made up only of Black—or colored—soldiers. These units' charges included protecting the expanding American West, serving in the Indian Wars, and serving in the Spanish-American War of 1898, during which the United States gained possession of Spanish territories in the Caribbean and the Pacific.

The lithograph at left depicts the storming of San Juan Hill, a key harbor position near the city of Santiago de Cuba. History records that the Rough Riders, under the direction of Lt. Col. Theodore Roosevelt, stormed this hill, won this battle, and contributed toward the United States' domination of Cuba. Critical to this victory were the battlefield contributions of the 24th and 25th Infantries.

"CHARGE OF THE 24TH AND 25TH COLORED INFANTRY AND RESCUE OF ROUGH RIDERS AT SAN JUAN HILL, JULY 2ND, 1898," by Kurz & Allison, Chicago, 1899. Color lithograph. Prints and Photographs.

THE
CREDO CALENDAR

"I believe in God who made of one blood all races that dwell on earth. I believe that all men, black and brown and white, are brothers, varying through Time and Opportunity, in form and gift and feature, but differing in no essential particular, and alike in soul and in the possibility of infinite development.

"Especially do I believe in the NEGRO RACE: in the beauty of its genius, the sweetness of its soul, and its strength in that meekness which shall yet inherit this turbulent earth.

"I believe in pride of race and lineage and self; in pride of self so deep as to scorn injustice to other selves; in pride of lineage so great as to despise no man's father; in pride of race so chivalrous as neither to offer bastardly to the weak nor beg wedlock of the strong, knowing that men may be brothers in Christ, even though they be not brothers-in-law.

"I believe in Service— humble, reverent service from the blackening of boots to the whitening of souls; for Work is Heaven, Idleness Hell, and Wage is the 'Well done!' of the Master who summoned all them that labor and are heavy laden, making no distinction between the black sweating cotton hands of Georgia and the First Families of Virginia; since all distinction not based on deed, is devilish and not divine.

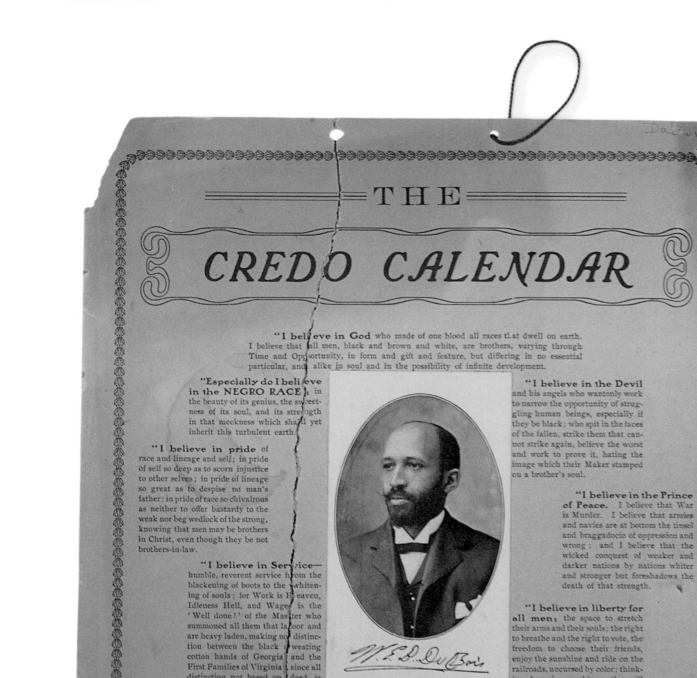

W. E. D. DuBois

"I believe in the Devil and his angels who wantonly work to narrow the opportunity of struggling human beings, especially if they be black; who spit in the faces of the fallen, strike them that cannot strike again, believe the worst and work to prove it, hating the image which their Maker stamped on a brother's soul.

"I believe in the Prince of Peace. I believe that War is Murder. I believe that armies and navies are at bottom the tinsel and braggadocio of oppression and wrong; and I believe that the wicked conquest of weaker and darker nations by nations whiter and stronger but foreshadows the death of that strength.

"I believe in liberty for all men: the space to stretch their arms and their souls; the right to breathe and the right to vote, the freedom to choose their friends, enjoy the sunshine and ride on the railroads, uncursed by color; thinking, dreaming, working as they will in a kingdom of God and love.

"I believe in the training of children black even as white; the leading out of little souls into the green pastures and beside the still waters, not for pelf or peace, but for Life lit by some large vision of beauty and goodness and truth; lest we forget, and the sons of the fathers, like Esau, for mere meat barter their birthright in a mighty nation.

. "Finally, I believe in Patience—

Patience with the weakness of the Weak and the strength of the Strong, the prejudice of the Ignorant and the ignorance of the Blind; patience with the tardy triumph of Joy and the mad chastening of Sorrow—patience with God."—W. E. B. DuBois.—N. Y. Independent.

1906		November				1906
SUN.	MON.	TUE.	WED.	THU.	FRI.	SAT.
				1	2	3
4	5	6	7	8	9	10
11	12	13	14	15	16	17
18	19	20	21	22	23	24
25	26	27	28	29	30	

THE CALENDAR PUBLISHING CO. BOSTON.

THE ROOTS OF THE NAACP. At the turn of the century, Black intellectuals debated the best way to gain full opportunity and justice in the United States. Some, such as Booker T. Washington—a leading educator and founder of the Tuskegee Institute—advocated gradual accommodation and slow economic advancement.

In 1905, 29 African-American men gathered, led by W. E. B. Du Bois, who had attended Harvard and the University of Berlin, and returned to the U.S. to fight for racial equality. Meeting at Niagara Falls, the group founded the Niagara Movement and rejected an accommodation policy.

A second meeting held in Harpers Ferry, West Virginia, in 1906 had more than 50 attendees, including women. They demanded the right to vote, the desegregation of public transportation, an end to discrimination, and equal rights.

In the long run, for lack of organization and funding, the Niagara Movement failed. Its members bonded with a group of white liberals, though, to form the National Association for the Advancement of Colored People in 1909.

The **NIAGARA MOVEMENT**

Second Annual Meeting

Storer College, Harper's Ferry, W. Va.

Aug. 15 to 19, 1906

Commemorating the 100th Birthday of John Brown and the Jubilee of the Battle of Ossawatomie.

(*OPPOSITE*) **THE CREDO CALENDAR,** by W. E. B. Du Bois, Boston, 1905. Calendar for 1906. Omnium Gatherum Collection.

(*LEFT*) **PROGRAM, THE NIAGARA MOVEMENT, SECOND ANNUAL MEETING,** 1906. Freeman Henry Morris Murray Papers.

WOMEN ATTENDING THE SECOND NIAGARA MOVEMENT CONFERENCE, photographer unknown, 1906. Freeman Henry Morris Murray Papers

BLACK VAUDEVILLE. Popular between the 1890s and the 1930s, stage vaudeville shows included magic, song and dance, acrobatics, juggling, and other entertainment acts. Antebellum minstrel shows featured whites who donned blackface and performed stereotyped song and dance routines. By the end of the century, though, many vaudeville and stock companies began to break away from the popular minstrel format. All-Black casts brought Black song and dance to the forefront.

Sisters Emma Louise and Anna Madah Hyers were the first Black musical comedy opera duo. Anna per-formed briefly in a musical written by Bert Williams and George Walker. A highly successful vaudeville comedy team, Williams and Walker in 1901 became the first Black recording artists. They also introduced a plot to the minstrel structure and pioneered the musical comedy form.

Vaudeville was also the venue that brought to life the ragtime music of composer Scott Joplin. The son of a slave, he created music that established a genre and brought Black traditions into the mainstream of popular American music.

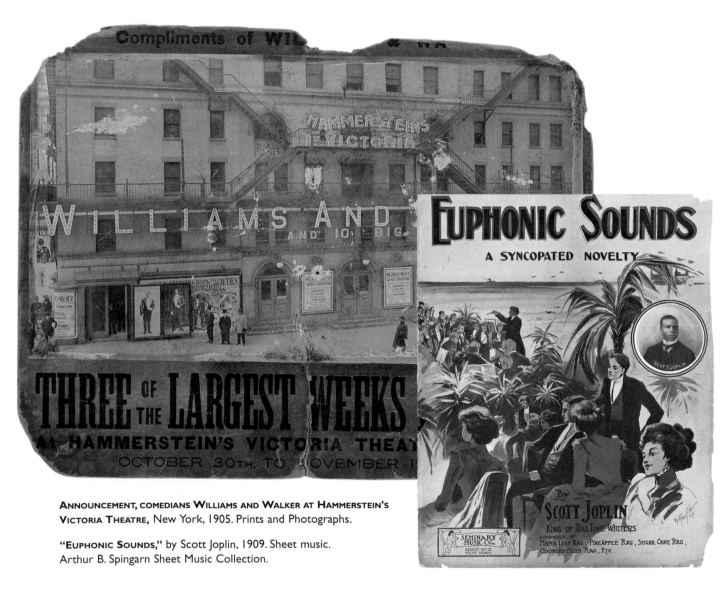

ANNOUNCEMENT, COMEDIANS WILLIAMS AND WALKER AT HAMMERSTEIN'S VICTORIA THEATRE, New York, 1905. Prints and Photographs.

"EUPHONIC SOUNDS," by Scott Joplin, 1909. Sheet music. Arthur B. Spingarn Sheet Music Collection.

(OPPOSITE) ANNA MADAH HYERS, photographer unknown, ca 1890. Prints and Photographs.

WORLD WAR I. On April 6, 1917, the U.S. declared war on Germany, marking its entry into World War I. Some 24 million men registered for the draft in the United States in 1917 and 1918. Roughly 31 percent of more than two million Black registrants for the draft were accepted.

Although the Army drafted both Black and white, they served in segregated units. Emmett J. Scott, former secretary to Booker T. Washington, was appointed special assistant to the secretary of war, advising him on problems stemming from segregation.

One of the problems addressed was that nothing was set up for the training of Negro officers. Following organized protests from the Black community, Fort Des Moines, Iowa, was designated as the site for the training camp.

Bands accompanied many Black regiments. Lt. James Reese Europe led the band of the 369th Infantry, also known as the Harlem Hellfighters. Sgt. Noble Sissle, who played with Europe before the war, joined him again, now as the band's drum major. Europe is credited with introducing jazz and ragtime to Europeans.

EUGENE DAVIDSON, HARRY KAZLOW, AND OLLIE LEWIS AT FORT DES MOINES, IOWA, photographer unknown, 1920. Eugene D. Davidson Collection.

(LEFT) **LT. JAMES REESE EUROPE STANDING IN FRONT OF TENT,** photographer unknown, ca 1918. Picture postcard. Ray Badger Collection.

(OPPOSITE) **HONORABLE DISCHARGE PAPERS, THOMAS W. TURNER,** 1918. Thomas Wyatt Turner Papers.

THIS CERTIFICATE OF HONOR

Is Presented To

Thomas W. Turner

On the Occasion of his Honorable Discharge from the Service of the United States, and

In recognition of
Loyal and Devoted Service as a

FOUR-MINUTE MAN

of the

COMMITTEE ON PUBLIC INFORMATION

During the War of
1917-1918

COMMITTEE ON PUBLIC INFORMATION

Secretary of State
Secretary of War
Secretary of Navy

CHAIRMAN

Given under our hand & seal this 24th day of December 1918 in the 143rd year of the Independence of the U.S.

NATIONAL DIRECTOR

COUNTERSIGNED BY LOCAL CHAIRMAN

THE KU KLUX KLAN. Jim Crow—named for a blackface minstrel show stereotype—was the name given to laws states established that systematically distanced Blacks from achieving full citizenship. The Jim Crow era roughly dates from the late 19th century up to World War II, when the desegregation of the Army marked the beginning of the end of legal segregation. Under Jim Crow, the races were separated in almost every aspect of public life. Efforts by African Americans to change their status or to challenge white supremacy were often answered with brutal acts of violence. During this period, more than 3,700 men and women were reported lynched in the United States.

The Ku Klux Klan, under whose watch many of the violent crimes were perpetrated, was first formed in 1866 in Pulaski, Tennessee. Made up of returning Confederate Army soldiers, the Klan at first was simply a fraternal organization. As it gained power and members, the organization violently opposed Reconstruction and the emancipation and of former slaves. The brutal acts of KKK members continued throughout Reconstruction until mass arrests diminished their activities.

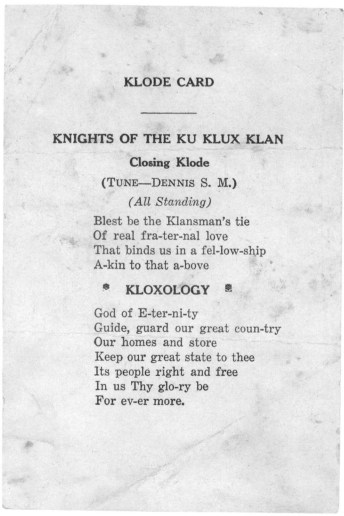

KLODE CARD, KNIGHTS OF THE KU KLUX KLAN, front and back, n.d. Omnium Gatherum Collection.

(*OPPOSITE*) **RURAL SCHOOL,** photograph taken by Charles Hamilton Houston during his travels through the South to study segregation and discrimination, 1930s. Charles Hamilton Houston Papers.

In 1915, on the 50th anniversary of the end of the Civil War and following the premiere of D. W. Griffith's film *Birth of a Nation* (originally titled *The Clansmen*), the KKK was reorganized in Georgia as the Knights of the Ku Klux Klan. Starting with 15 members, the organization grew to 85,000 by the fall of 1921 as the result of a vigorous membership drive. No longer only a southern rural phenomenon, the KKK formed chapters in northern cities such as Chicago and New York, where many southern Blacks had migrated.

The KKK agenda was multifaceted. It harmonized with Jim Crow laws and claimed to safeguard American ideals and values. Attacks spread, with targets widened and tactics going beyond physical violence. Catholics, for example, were accused of pledging their allegiance to the pope rather than to the United States, and a Klan pamphlet campaign attempted to undermine Catholic influence on politics and society, particularly education. The Klan worked to elect its members into political positions, both local and national. Peaking in power in 1929, the Klan declined in membership after the Internal Revenue Service came after the organization for owing back taxes totaling more than half a million dollars.

THE MOENS AFFAIR: WASHINGTON BETWEEN THE WARS

BETWEEN THE OUTBREAK OF WORLD WAR I in 1914 and the 1919 race riot in Washington, D.C., a scandal contributed to Washington's escalating racial tensions. A visiting Dutch scientist named Herman Moens used photographs of young African Americans, mostly nude women, to support his theory that persons of mixed black and white parentage combined the best attributes of both races. The study earned him the label of spy and led to his subsequent arrest on obscenity charges. The Moens Affair, as it was tagged by the press, embodied the nation's struggle with foreigners and persons of color and with the social and biological mixing of races.

Born in Holland in 1875, zoologist Herman Bernelot Moens in April 1914 came to Los Angeles, where he came in contact with the African-American community and developed a theory that scientifically guided mixed marriages would produce the perfect human specimen. After several excursions to Cuba and Panama, Moens returned to the States in 1916, settling in Washington, D.C., and embarking on a study of light-complected youths. He showed photographs from earlier studies to the director of the Smithsonian Institution, who was so impressed that he provided photographers and studio space. Moens befriended Charlotte Hunter, a young, unmarried Black woman who taught at the Minor Normal School for Colored Children. She later alleged that she brought young students to his studio at his request, but only with the permission or accompaniment of their parents.

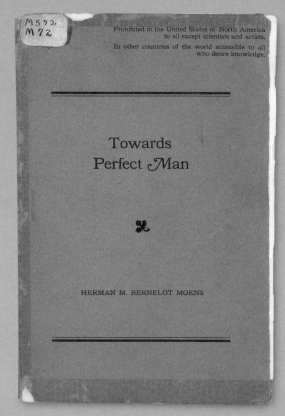

Moens attracted the attention of the Bureau of Investigation (today's FBI), which, because he was a foreigner with no visible means of support who socialized with Black citizens in Jim Crow Washington while openly discussing the benefits of mixed marriage, suspected him of being a spy. On October 25, 1918, while he was detained on suspicion of spying, the bureau confiscated his papers, books, pamphlets, and notes, charging him with obscenity. He was convicted on April 1, 1919.

Moens was forced to remain in the U.S. for three more years. After returning to Europe, he published an explanation of his research and his Washington experience, titled *Towards Perfect Man: Contributions to Somatological and Philosophical Anthropology*. In 1928 he helped found the Society of Universal Brotherhood, then departed to start his own group, the Supra Nation. Until he died in 1938 in Morocco, Moens continued to fight against racism and for nationalism. —*Donna M. Wells, Howard University*

TOWARDS PERFECT MAN, by Herman M. Bernelot Moens, 1922. Library Collection.

(*OPPOSITE*) **MOENS WITH TWO SCHOOLCHILDREN,** photographer unknown, published in *Towards Perfect Man,* 1922.

WORLD WAR II. When America entered World War II in 1941, more than 2.5 million African-American men had registered for the draft. The discrimination shown Blacks in World War I was not forgotten, however, and it served to mobilize soldiers to press for better treatment and working conditions.

Unwilling to serve again in a segregated army, hundreds of thousands of Black Americans threatened to march on Washington in 1941. Leading them in their mission was Asa Philip Randolph, a labor union spokesman who had gained fame by organizing the Pullman porters in their quest for better pay and work conditions on the railroad. In response to the threatened march, President Roosevelt issued an executive order that reemphasized the policy of full participation in the military.

On the civilian front, Lucy Diggs Slowe Hall was built at the corner of Third and U Streets, N.W., in Washington, to serve as housing for unmarried Black women working for the government during the war. It was named for Howard University's first dean of women, Lucy Diggs Slowe.

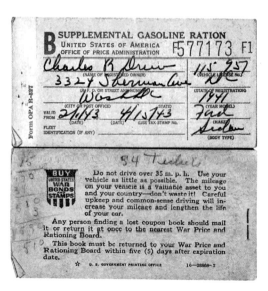

GAS RATIONING CARD BELONGING TO CHARLES R. DREW, Office of Price Administration, 1943. Charles R. Drew Papers.

CLARA CAMILLE CARROLL, GOVERNMENT WORKER, Office of War Information, ca 1941. Prints and Photographs.

(OPPOSITE) **"KEEP US FLYING!"** Artist unknown, sponsored by Office of War Information, 1943. Buy War Bonds poster showing Tuskegee Airman Lt. Robert W. Diez of the 99th Pursuit Squadron. Prints and Photographs.

CHAPTER 9
The New Negro
1920-1939

In the last decade something beyond the watch and guard of statistics has happened in the life of the American Negro and the three norns [goddesses of fate] who have traditionally presided over the Negro problem have a changeling in their laps. The Sociologist, the Philanthropist, the Race-leader are not unaware of the New Negro but they are at a loss to account for him. He simply cannot be swathed in their formulae. For the younger generation is vibrant with a new psychology; the new spirit is awake in the masses, and under the very eyes of the professional observers is transforming what has been a perennial problem into the progressive phases of contemporary Negro life.

Alain Locke, 1925
"Enter the New Negro," in *Survey Graphic,*
Harlem Number

1920 - 1939

The spirit in the Black community between the world wars was decidedly different from that of the years before World War I. A new militant leadership had by then begun to rise, including Carter G. Woodson and W. E. B. Du Bois, who inspired confidence and self-assertiveness. They continued the struggle for full citizenship but encouraged self-respect and self-awareness in their writings about Black people and their culture.

It was the publication of the Harlem Number of the Survey Graphic magazine in 1925, though, that outlined the progressive spirit embodied in the visual, performing, and literary arts coming from young Black artists. This period was known by different names including the Harlem Renaissance, the New Negro Movement, the New Negro Renaissance, and the Black Renaissance Movement. Whatever it was called, it could not be defined geographically, since this cultural awakening was evident in urban areas across the country, anywhere there had recently been a large influx of Black residents.

Alain Locke, a professor of philosophy at Howard University at the time, is considered the architect of the Renaissance and the force behind the new aesthetic, which was deeply rooted in Black folk culture.

THE GREAT MIGRATION

THE GREAT MIGRATION OF AFRICAN AMERICANS from the southern states of the United States to the North and West is a significant theme of 20th-century American history. In 1900 about 90 percent of the African-American population lived in the South—the states of the old Confederacy—and in the border states of Delaware, Maryland, Kentucky, and Missouri. By 1970, only half remained there. The reasons for this population shift are numerous. The boll weevil brought on crop failures, which resulted in a dramatic drop in the South's economy during the early 1900s. Terrorism perpetrated by white supremacist groups like the Ku Klux Klan was equally influential. Perhaps most important was the lure of better jobs and salaries in the North, especially in cities like New York, Chicago, Detroit, and Pittsburgh. As American industry increased production during World Wars I and II, the call for workers became urgent. African Americans joined a general population of Southerners in the movement northward.

The story begins in the late 19th century, when African Americans reached perhaps the lowest point in their struggle for civil and human rights. The reforms of the Reconstruction era following the Civil War disappeared in the wake of growing anti-Black violence in the South and indifference to African-American rights nationwide. Decisions by the U.S. Supreme Court gutted the civil rights legislation that had been passed to protect Black citizens recently freed from slavery. The Supreme

"RUG CUTTERS" (couple dancing the cakewalk), by Richmond Barthé, 1939. Bronze. General Museum Collection.

Court's conservative interpretations of the Reconstruction amendments to the Constitution soon erased citizenship and voting rights for former slaves.

BLACK LABOR WAS THE FOUNDATION of the southern economy. The thought of losing it was traumatic to the region's landed elite. Therefore, the violent and repressive policies of the post-Reconstruction South were aimed at replicating slavery as nearly as possible. Even the best efforts of Black leaders, who proposed a compromise with white supremacists, did little to stem the tide of public lynchings and other atrocities against Black people. Booker T. Washington's campaign to expand Black education and economic growth while postponing equal civil rights ultimately left the larger issues of human and civil rights unresolved.

Between 1900 and 1920 the African-American populations of New York City and Chicago increased dramatically. New York City's Harlem became a destination of choice for more than 100,000 newcomers, including Black intellectuals and artists, as well as workers from the South and the Caribbean. Consequently, Harlem became the center of a renaissance that featured an impressive growth in the creative production of literature and music. As the nation's media capital, New York City offered an opportunity to export the products of Black talent to the entire nation and the world. Creative artists like Langston Hughes, Duke Ellington, Zora Neale Hurston, Bessie Smith, and Louis Armstrong found new venues for their work.

Chicago was also an important terminus for Black migration. In this case, the new jazz music worked its way up the Mississippi River from New Orleans to Kansas City and Memphis, then finally to Chicago, where the city's South Side—the economic and entertainment district of which was known as The Stroll—teemed with cultural and political activity. Perhaps for the first time since Jamestown, Black Americans were tasting the fruits of free expression in an environment that was relatively unfettered.

Black newspapers with nationwide circulations, like Robert Vann's *Pittsburgh Courier* and Robert Abbott's *Chicago Defender* (which was distributed to its many readers south of the Mason-Dixon Line by Black Pullman porters), trumpeted the details of southern lynchings on their front pages as often as they could. They offered by way of contrast descriptions of northern cities that promised a better life, including better wages and safety from terror.

Of course, the North proved to be no heaven. Black newcomers were often funneled into overcrowded inner cities where housing was old and city services were scarce. Housing discrimination coupled with ever decreasing job opportunities established ghettos that provided sources of cheap labor and created victims for organized crime. Tensions between Blacks and poor whites, especially recent immigrants, were quite apparent in the urban North throughout the period of Black migration. As if to make the point even clearer, race riots broke out in Chicago and Detroit in 1919. In Chicago, three days of violence began when a Black boy inadvertently swam into a segregated area at a public beach, only to be stoned and subsequently drowned. Poet Carl Sandburg, at the time a young reporter, was assigned to write a series of articles on the riots that were later collected into book form.

Black organizations moved to confront the challenges of Jim Crow—legalized racial discrimination—in the South and economic discrimination in the North. A racially integrated group of progressive activists that included the famous Black intellectual W. E. B. Du Bois founded the National Association for the Advancement of Colored People in 1909. The next year brought the National Urban League. Both organizations attacked the problems of the legal status and economic situation of Blacks.

By 1920 there were other groups in the mix. The largest was the Universal Negro Improvement Association (UNIA), founded in his homeland by Jamaican-born Marcus Garvey and then transplanted to New York City. Garvey's theme of Black nationalism, which included an emphasis on Black self-esteem and the liberation of Africa from colonial rule, attracted the largest membership of any contemporary Black organization. Chapters and divisions of the UNIA reached phenomenal numbers, with more than 700 in the United States alone, and branches in Canada, the Caribbean and Latin America, Africa, Europe, and Australia. Smaller but nevertheless significant groups included the Marxist-oriented African Blood Brotherhood and the Moorish American Science Temple, a precursor to the Nation of Islam. All of these organizations appealed to Black immigrants from the South and the Caribbean who sought comprehensive solutions to the political and economic problems facing the Black world.

THE MIGRATION HAD AN IMPORTANT EFFECT on activism among African-American women. The Black migration to Kansas and Oklahoma in the 1880s and 1890s was in part the result of newspaper editor Ida B. Wells's clarion call to leave the post-Reconstruction South and move west. By 1895 Black women were organizing around the nation in support of equal civil rights for the entire race and for women. They met in conventions in Boston, Washington, and Chicago to devise strategies opposing the defamation of African-American women in the press and other media.

Wells took the lead in the fight against compromising civil rights for Blacks and condemned lynching in the strongest terms. In the northern cities that became the destinations for many women seeking jobs, African-American women's organizations provided housing and employment services and child care facilities. Indeed, the National Urban League grew out of a coalition of these Black women's organizations in urban America. The movement north slowed down in the 1930s, during the Depression, but increased when World War II began. As factory jobs opened up in the North, mechanization came to the cotton fields, displacing many black farmers.

This great migration of Black men and women ended in the 1970s, and many of them began to return to the nation's southern Sunbelt. By that time, though, an estimated six million blacks had migrated from the South, and many of America's largest and most important cities—including Chicago, New York City, Detroit, Philadelphia, Washington, D.C., and Los Angeles—had large Black populations. In the end, the large shifts in population had created a new America—a nation with an African-American population spread in significant numbers from coast to coast.
—*Emory Joel Tolbert, Howard University*

THE RIVERSIDE GOLF CLUB ÷ 1924
WASHINGTON, DC   Scurlock, Photo.

RIVERSIDE GOLF CLUB, detail of panorama on National Mall by Scurlock Studios, 1924. The Riverside Golf Club organized the first

African-American tournament in the country in 1924 in Washington, D.C. Prints and Photographs.

PERFORMING ARTS. Although the Renaissance is considered primarily a literary and intellectual movement, performance artists contributed significantly to the new perspective on Black folk art as well. Dancers, composers, acrobats, theater artists, musical comics, and other stage actors explored Black themes and included Blacks at all production levels.

The 1921 production of *Shuffle Along,* for example, featured an all-Black cast and was the first Broadway musical to be written, produced, and performed by Blacks. This review also introduced such rising young stars as Paul Ro-beson and 15-year-old singer and dancer Josephine Baker.

Some entertainers, such as dancer Mae Olden and multiple-act entertainers like the Bruce Stock Company, performed in theaters on the Black vaudeville circuit, while others, such as the Nicholas Brothers, skyrocketed to fame.

Fayard Nicholas and his younger brother, Harold, grew up watching the great Black vaudeville acts, and were inspired by dancers such as Bill Robinson and Alice Whitman. As Fayard Nicholas later recalled, "One day at the Standard Theatre in Philadelphia, I looked onstage and thought, 'They're having fun up there; I'd like to do

(RIGHT) **MAE OLDEN,** photographer unknown, 1917. Harry Bowman Collection of Vaudeville and Gospel Photographs.

NICHOLAS BROTHERS, photographer unknown, circa 1935. Autographed to Thelma Greene. Thelma Greene Theater Collection.

something like that.'" And they did that and more. Their unique dancing abilities, combining smooth tap and a dizzying array of acrobatic spins, twists, and flips, boosted them to fame from an early age, and by 1932, when they were 18 and 11, respectively, they were playing the Cotton Club in Harlem. As child performers they were the only entertainers in the all African-American cast allowed to mingle with patrons.

In the 1920s, the blues became a major element in African-American and American music. Lovie Austin, born Cora Calhoun, was a popular figure in the Chicago jazz and blues scene, becoming one of the first important jazz band leaders. Pianist Mary Lou Williams remembers "seeing this great woman sitting in the pit" at the Theatre Owner Bookers Association Theatre in Pittsburgh, "conducting a group of five or six men...playing the show with her left hand and writing music with her right. Wow!"

Publicity portraits of better known artists are abundant, but the richest material found in collections features obscure artists hardly known today but who still made an impact of the spreading of Black influence into mainstream American arts.

BRUCE'S STOCK COMPANY, photographer unknown, 1919. Harry Bowman Collection of Vaudeville and Gospel Photographs.

(INSET) **"BLEEDING HEARTED BLUES,"** by Lovie Austin, 1923. Sheet music. Arthur B. Spingarn Sheet Music Collection.

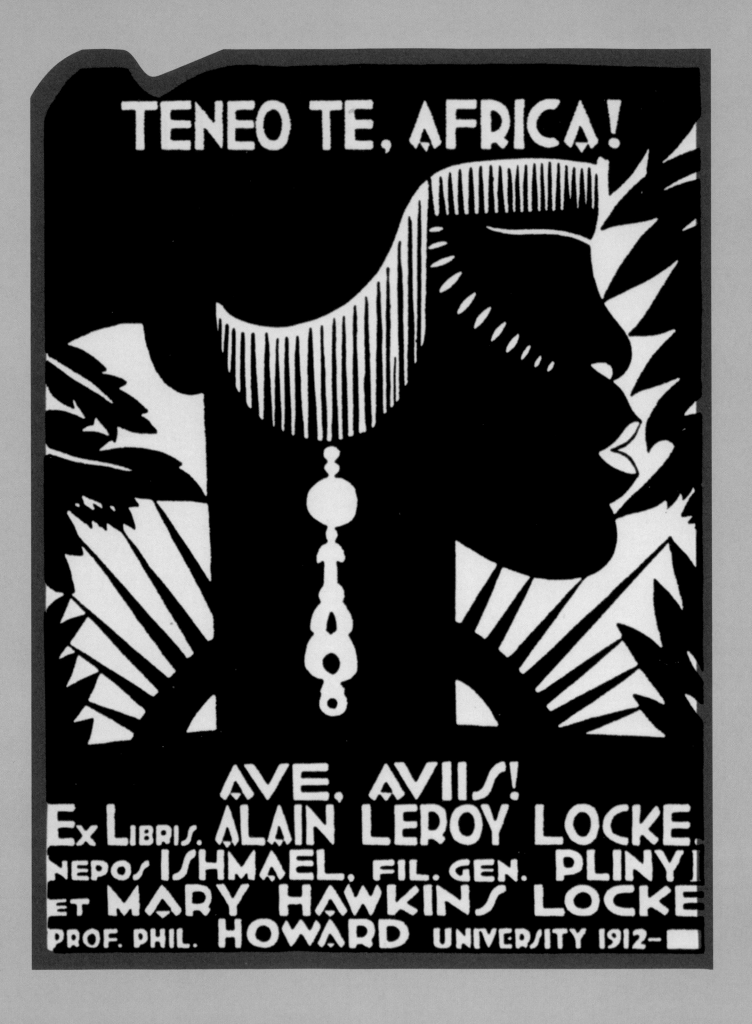

ALAIN LOCKE

ALAIN LOCKE IS KNOWN PRIMARILY as the intellectual who orchestrated the Harlem Renaissance, the Black literary and visual arts movement of the 1920s. In *The New Negro: An Interpretation* (1925), often called the bible of the movement, Locke pulled together writing from Jean Toomer, Claude McKay, Langston Hughes, and Countee Cullen; social commentary from W. E. B. Du Bois, James Weldon Johnson, and Elise Johnson McDougald; and illustrations from German artist Winold Reiss and African-American illustrator Aaron Douglas. The result, an anthology of spectacular richness, symbolized the beauty of the modern Black urban experience and of the figure Locke defined as the New Negro. After that, Locke became a lightning rod for Black intellectual life. He had defined a movement.

But Locke was much more than an intellectual kingpin of the Harlem Renaissance. He was the first African-American Rhodes Scholar and the first African American to earn a Ph.D. in philosophy from Harvard University; a Howard University professor for almost 40 years; a prolific literary, drama, and music critic; an art historian and curator of African and African-American art; a race theorist; and a diasporic intellectual who worked tirelessly to knit together the cultural aspirations of Africans, West Indians, and African Americans. He founded the Howard Players, a Black theater group that performed, among other works, Eugene O'Neill's *Emperor Jones*. With his colleague Montgomery Gregory, he founded the *Stylus* literary magazine, to which Zora Neale Hurston contributed while a student at Howard.

As a mover and shaker in the first half of the 20th century, not only was Locke influential, he was infamous, engaging in intellectual and personal battles with rivals such as Du Bois and Hurston. He also made numerous alliances with white patrons, some of which led to bitter feelings, as was the case in his struggle with Albert Barnes, the wealthy Pennsylvania art collector and iconoclast. Yet Locke always found time to help others, especially young people. The support that he offered a fellow Black gay writer named James Baldwin comes through poignantly in their brief correspondence.

No ivory tower scholar, Locke was a public intellectual who believed it his duty—and the duty of all educated people—to take on the task of increasing one's sophistication, knowledge, and humanity through culture. He sought to create a model of ethical living that combined the spiritual and the social. He lived out his commitment to leave the Earth a better place for humanity than he found it. —*Jeffrey C. Stewart, George Mason University*

ALAIN LOCKE AT HOME, photographer unknown, n.d. Alain Locke Papers.

(OPPOSITE) **TENEO TE, AFRICA!**, bookplate design by Aaron Douglass for Alain Locke, ca 1920. Alain Locke Papers.

LANGSTON HUGHES. James Langston Hughes was often called the poet laureate of the Black people. In his renowned poem "I, Too, Sing America" (a response to American icon Walt Whitman) Hughes reflects the conflicted feelings of many Blacks in the days after World War I. They took great pride in their American citizenship but felt deep anguish in being denied all that should come with it. The story behind the writing of the poem illustrates the ironic battle for democracy during those postwar years.

In 1924, aboard a transatlantic freighter, Hughes jumped ship to France and Italy. On a train back to Paris from Genoa, Italy, he fell asleep and was robbed of his passport and most of his money. Stranded, he found cheap accommodations, worked odd jobs, and befriended a number of foreigners who helped him as much as they could. He sought work on a freighter bound for the United States but was denied a job because of his color.

Depressed, on September 25, 1924, Hughes wrote a letter to his friend Alain Locke in which he explained that he had no more paper but still wanted to share his most recent poem. He wrote "I, Too" on the back of the letter, reflecting his desire to be judged on his merit and not the color of his skin. Finally, the captain of a ship with an all-Black crew agreed to sign Langston Hughes on to work for passage but no pay.

On March 1, 1925, "I, Too, Sing America" was first published in *Survey Graphic* magazine, in the special issue devoted to the arts of the Black Renaissance and edited by Locke.

LETTER TO ALAIN LOCKE FROM LANGSTON HUGHES WITH ORIGINAL POEM "I, TOO," September 25, 1924. Alain Locke Papers.

(OPPOSITE) **LANGSTON HUGHES,** photograph by James Latimer Allen, ca 1927. Alain Locke Papers.

A. PHILIP RANDOLPH
INTERNATIONAL PRESIDENT

MILTON P. WEBSTER
1ST INTERNATIONAL VICE-PRESIDENT
4231 SOUTH MICHIGAN AVENUE
CHICAGO, ILLINOIS

BENNIE SMITH
2ND INTERNATIONAL VICE-PRESIDENT
2611-13 MICHIGAN AVENUE
DETROIT, MICHIGAN

ASHLEY L. TOTTEN
INTERNATIONAL SECRETARY-TREASURER

E. J. BRADLEY
3RD INTERNATIONAL VICE-PRESIDENT
11 NORTH JEFFERSON STREET
ST. LOUIS, MISSOURI

C. L. DELLUMS
4TH INTERNATIONAL VICE-PRESIDENT
1716 SEVENTH STREET
OAKLAND, CALIFORNIA

BROTHERHOOD *of* **SLEEPING CAR PORTERS**

TRAIN, CHAIR CAR, COACH PORTERS AND ATTENDANTS

AN INTERNATIONAL UNION
AFFILIATED WITH THE A. F. OF L.

217 WEST 125TH STREET
(ROOM 301)
MO 2-5080-1

NIGHTS, SUNDAYS AND HOLIDAYS
UNiversity 4-8262

440

April 26th, 1941

Dr. Herbert C. Marshall
1011 You Street, N. W.
Washington, D. C.

Dear Friend:

      I plan to hold a meeting at the YMCA on Wednesday,
April 30th, at 6:30 pm, for the purpose of discussing with a few Negro
citizens of Washington the question of mobilizing thousands of Negroes
to march on Washington in the interest of jobs in national defense.

      It is my hope that such a demonstration may be so
powerful as to bring such pressure upon the President to cause him to
give serious consideration to the issuance of an executive order to ban
discrimination against Negroes in all government departments and national defense.

      Our Mr. W. S. Anderson, President of the Washington
Division of the Brotherhood of Sleeping Car Porters, informed me that
he either talked with you or attempted to get in touch with you by tele-
phone to advise you of our desire to have you attend this meeting.

      I hope it may be convenient for you to attend this
meeting.

      With cordial good wishes, I am

      Very sincerely yours,

A. Philip Randolph
International President

apr/mf

ORGANIZING. With the continued exclusion of Blacks from American society and the increasing need for them to protect any rights they had successfully obtained, organizing was crucial. Some organizations that had been founded in years prior expanded their missions in the 20th century, while new organizations formed to address contemporary issues and needs, such as Black entrepreneurship.

For example, the Brotherhood of Sleeping Car Porters was organized in 1925 to negotiate with the Pullman Company, at the time the largest employer of Blacks in the nation. The National Association of Colored Women, established in 1896, became a strong voice advocating woman suffrage. Banks run by and for Blacks dated from the 1880s, and Richard Wright founded the National Negro Bankers Association in the 1890s. All these organizations addressed the social challenges facing Black businesspeople and their communities, but a positive focus on education, leadership opportunities, and racial advancement for all Black Americans remained at the core of their efforts.

"**PRESIDENTS OF THE NATIONAL ASSOCIATION OF COLORED WOMEN, 1895-1920,**" ca 1920. Poster. Prints and Photographs.

(RIGHT) **BADGE BELONGING TO RICHARD R. WRIGHT, NATIONAL NEGRO BANKERS ASSOCIATION CONFERENCE,** 1930. Maj. Richard Robert Wright, Sr., Family Papers.

(BELOW) **YMCA BUTTON,** 1923. Jesse E. Moorland Papers.

(OPPOSITE) **LETTER FROM A. PHILIP RANDOLPH, PRESIDENT OF THE BROTHERHOOD OF SLEEPING CAR PORTERS, TO HERBERT C. MARSHALL,** April 26, 1941. NAACP-D.C. Branch Papers.

THE GREAT DEPRESSION. The worldwide economic downturn known as the Great Depression began in the United States with the 1929 stock market crash and lasted through most of the 1930s. In 1930, at least 50 percent of the Black working population, in both the North and the South, was unemployed.

A corner of 170th Street in New York was known as the Bronx Slave Market. There, unemployed domestics and laborers would come each morning, seeking day work for which they might be paid 20 or 30 cents an hour.

Financial relief was available to some through the federally funded Works Progress Administration (WPA), which employed Americans in a variety of jobs around the country.

The creativity of many African-American artists and historians was encouraged during the short period that WPA was in existence, and many continued their creative work even after federal funding ended. Part of the WPA, the Federal Writers' Project supported research and writing about African-American lives and times. One of the most comprehensive results of that project was *The Negro in Virginia*, a volume of Black history in Virginia from colonial times up to the early 20th century, illustrated with photographs taken especially for the book.

PRODUCTS OF THE "SLAVE MARKET." LIFE GOES HARD IN SPITE OF HOPES. THE YOUTH SEEKS JOB AS WINDOW-WASHER.

"MAKE A WISH. BRONX SLAVE MARKET, 170TH STREET, NEW YORK," photograph by Robert M. McNeill. *Flash!* magazine, February 14, 1938.

(OPPOSITE) **"SPRING PLANTING,"** photograph by Robert H. McNeill, 1938. From *The Negro in Virginia* (1940), Federal Writers' Project, Works Progress Administration. Walter E. Waring Papers.

THE NEW NEGRO ALLIANCE. "Don't Buy Where You Can't Work!" was the slogan of the New Negro Alliance (NNA), an organization remembered for boycotts and protests staged to gain employment and increase consumer power for Blacks in the 1930s and 1940s. NNA leaders theorized that organizations like the National Business League and the NAACP were fighting the symptoms, not the disease, and that even in Depression times, organized buying could shift power into Black hands. Formed in 1933 in Washington, D.C., the NNA campaigned against stores in Black neighborhoods that did not hire Black workers. Activist and educator Mary McLeod Bethune was a protester against People's Drug Store at 14th and U Streets.

In the landmark 1938 Supreme Court case of *New Negro Alliance* v. *Sanitary Grocery*, the court upheld the NNA's right to boycott a business that was not employing Blacks: Soon similar groups sprang up across the country. The New Negro Alliance disbanded in 1940.

"NEGROES EMPLOYED AS A RESULT OF NNA," photograph by Robert H. McNeill, ca 1940. Eugene C. Davidson Collection.

(LEFT) **"TO ALL FAIR-MINDED PEOPLE,"** New Negro Alliance Leaflet, ca 1935. Eugene C. Davidson Collection.

NEW NEGRO ALLIANCE
YEAR BOOK

1939

■

First Edition

■

Washington
District of Columbia

- - - - TWENTY-FIVE CENTS THE COPY - - - -

NEW NEGRO ALLIANCE YEARBOOK, edited by Eugene Davidson, 1939. Leon Ransom Papers.

CHAPTER 10

Civil Rights

1941-1968

Britton: Now, there has been a story—and I want to get it from you if it's true—that you did not stand because your feet were tired. Is that correct?

Parks: Well, no that isn't correct, but that was a popular saying. I actually had worked all day and it was very logical that could have been true. But I don't know where the saying began. I didn't tell anyone that my feet were hurting. It was just popular, I suppose, because they wanted to give some excuse other than the fact that I didn't want to be pushed around. I didn't feel like I was being treated fairly. And I had been working for a long time—a number of years, in fact—to be treated as a human being with dignity…not only for myself, but all those who were being mistreated, to have a chance for equality in whatever phase of life we may find ourselves.

Rosa Parks, September 28, 1967
Interview with John H. Britton
Civil Rights Documentation Project

1941-1968   *The struggle for civil rights, a citizen's legal and constitutional rights, began long before the 1960s. Amendments to the Constitution and small local battles slowly over the years eroded the legal system that barred Blacks from enjoying full civil rights. In some places, social segregation was practiced when legal segregation was not enforced.*

Brown v. Board of Education of Topeka, Kansas, decided by the Supreme Court in 1954, is considered the case that began to dismantle legal segregation. It brought together five discrimination suits being filed across the country against locally segregated school systems where the Black schools were found to be inadequate. While attorneys Charles Hamilton Houston, James Nabrit, Thurgood Marshall, and others mounted challenges in court, the American public put pressure on local, state, and federal governments for economic and social equality. Fraternal, civic, militant, professional, and grassroots organizations were created to fill the void when community needs were not met. They, and individuals like Rosa Parks, brought national and international attention to the condition of Black America. Documents and images record daily events during this period, while oral interviews give glimpses into the lives of those at the center of the struggle.

POLITICAL PHILOSOPHY OF THE CIVIL RIGHTS MOVEMENT

THE CIVIL RIGHTS MOVEMENT changed the course of American history and redefined acceptable patterns of race relations in society. It sought to redefine the meaning of democracy, citizenship, and social justice, and to realign the role of government and power with respect to race relations in the U.S.

From its inception as a system of colonies, the United States had embedded at the core of its societal formation a fundamental contradiction. The founding fathers professed the values of liberty, equality, and fraternity, yet they conceived of the United States as a white man's country, a haven for descendants of Europe. Consequently, they propagated systemic racism by enslavement of Africans and subjugation and genocide against the indigenous people of the Americas. Before the advent of the civil rights movement, American society was quartered by de jure segregation based on the power of law and by de facto segregation based on the force of custom and a culture of racial preference. The civil rights movement confronted this central contradiction in American life.

The civil rights era, one of the most important periods in African-American history, is also acknowledged as a critical stage in 20th-century American social history. The movement is indelibly etched in the national memory through significant events forever associated with the celebrated campaigns opposed to racial segregation: Mrs. Rosa Parks's refusal to surrender her seat to a white male passenger, sparking the boycott of the public bus system in Montgomery, Alabama; the 1954 Supreme

UNTITLED POSTER SHOWING CIVIL RIGHTS LEADERS, by George Bx. Stewart, n.d. E. Ethelbert Miller Poster Collection.

Court decision in *Brown* v. *Board of Education of Topeka, Kansas*, which outlawed segregation in public schools; the sit-in at Woolworth's lunch counter by students from Shaw University in Raleigh, North Carolina, to protest the restaurant's refusal to serve Black customers; and the protest demonstrations led by Dr. Martin Luther King, Jr., and his organization, the Southern Christian Leadership Conference (SCLC), and by the youthful organizers of the Student Nonviolent Coordinating Committee (SNCC) and the Congress of Racial Equality (CORE). These events were important milestones in the long journey for freedom undertaken by the descendants of enslaved Africans, but they were not the first steps of the struggle for civil rights.

THE CONSTITUTION DID NOT EXTEND political inclusion or rights as citizens to Africans, yet free Africans in the 18th century petitioned the colonial governments of Massachusetts, New York, and Pennsylvania to protect their rights in civil society. Moreover, in pursuit of freedom and basic social and political rights, almost 200,000 free Africans in the North volunteered with the Union Army, and many more deserted the South during the same war years. Leaders such as Paul Cuffee, David Walker, Maria Stewart, Frederick Douglass, Martin Delaney, Harriett Tubman, and Ida B. Wells dedicated their lives to the fight for human rights for Black people.

After emancipation, plantation owners and merchant elites created a new racial hierarchy with patterns of social relations that denied recently emancipated Africans all political rights, economic freedom, social justice, and human dignity. Former slave owners and their allies tried mightily to reconstitute their control over African labor through a modified version of slavery by enacting a series of segregation laws, known as the Black Codes, and an economic system based on cotton production, tenant farming, and sharecropping. By 1880 every Southern state had fewer but larger plantations. The control of both land and labor was more concentrated, and the relationship between political and economic power in a racist system was apparent.

In the aftermath of the Civil War, during the short-lived Reconstruction period of 1865 to 1880, an American foundation for civil rights began to take shape, in the form of the three critical constitutional amendments: the 13th, which declared the end of slavery; the 14th, granting citizenship to former slaves; and the 15th, conferring on ex-slaves the right to vote. These amendments set the ground for the protracted struggle for civil rights that would extend from the 19th deep into the 20th century. The National Association for the Advancement of Colored People (NAACP) was founded to spearhead the legal strategy for civil rights; the Universal Negro Improvement Association (the Garvey Movement) emphasized the denial of civil rights for Black people on an international scale. Radical intellectuals and artists of the Harlem Renaissance denounced racism and demanded guarantees for civil rights. Militant unionists such as A. Philip Randolph and the Brotherhood of Sleeping Car Porters exposed the exploitation of Black workers and sharecroppers and threatened the first march on Washington unless the federal government desegregated the military and federal hiring.

The civil rights movement of the 20th century was created and led by Black people with the expressed intention to challenge and transform the structure of racism and southern politics, and by extension northern politics as well. Civil rights organizers encountered entrenched hostility, systematic resistance, economic reprisals, and unmitigated violence in the form of bombings, shootings, beatings, mob attacks, and targeted killings.

The civil rights movement did not emerge in a vacuum. It relied on traditional African-American institutions. Masonic lodges and women's clubs, fraternities and sororities, religious denominations, and historically Black colleges and universities provided financial and logistical leadership along with community and political support. The African-American church was especially vital to the success of the movement. Churches offered sanctuary for public meetings, space for planning sessions and training classes, and venues to recruit participants.

Two components made up the civil rights movement. On one side was the older NAACP and its methodical, disciplined legal program of calculated lawsuits challenging segregation law. The legal strategy of the NAACP was developed at Howard University Law School by Charles Hamilton Houston, a brilliant legal theorist, and a group of his best students, including Thurgood Marshall, who would become the first African-American U.S. Supreme Court Justice. Marshall had applied to attend law school at the University of Maryland. Refused because of race, he attended Howard instead. As director of the NAACP Legal Defense Fund, he was the lead attorney on a team of four who argued *Brown* v. *Board of Education* before the Supreme Court. The legal victory in this case accelerated opposition to segregation and was pivotal to the legal impetus for civil rights. On the other side of the movement, a more militant campaign was led by SNCC, CORE, and SCLC, rooted in the philosophy of nonviolence and the praxis of civil disobedience. These activists complemented the more moderate NAACP approach with their tactics of picketing, freedom rides, sit-ins, protest marches, mass demonstrations, and economic boycotts.

From 1930 to 1970, the struggle for civil rights cohered into a national social movement. The span between the 1954 *Brown* decision and the 1965 Voting Rights Act is considered the time frame of the 20th-century civil rights movement. Though primarily focused in the South, civil rights actions took place in major industrial northern states as well. Many civil rights workers in the South were recruited from college campuses, clergy, and unions in the North. Young people were at the forefront of the movement, prime movers in civil disobedience tactics that dramatized noncompliance with Supreme Court rulings on segregation and leveraged political pressure on the legislature and the President.

In its effort to define a nonracial democracy, the civil rights movement had broad domestic and international influence. It presented a new paradigm of democratic rights—that all citizens have the same rights, without prejudice as to race, gender, ethnicity, class, or previous status of servitude—and established civil rights as a principle of constitutional law. Internationally, the civil rights movement shared a common cause with anticolonialism struggles and independence movements in Africa and the Caribbean. Malcolm X and Martin Luther King, Jr., have become transnational political figures, and the signature song of the U.S. civil rights movement, "We Shall Overcome," has become an international anthem for social justice movements. By changing the course of history in the U.S., the civil rights movement went a long way to define the future of the world. —*James Turner, Cornell University*

EARLY YEARS OF THE MOVEMENT. Between the end of World War II and the passing of the Civil Rights Act in 1964, many Black entertainers devoted their lives to fighting social injustices. Entertainment became an important means of connecting and communicating with mass audiences. Negro Freedom Rallies, for example, began in the mid-1940s, at the height of the war. Yearly rallies featured Black musicians and dancers as well as civic leaders. Posters and programs proudly displayed the star-studded cast of participants. Pearl Primus danced before a sellout audience of 5,000 at the first rally, held in New York City at Madison Square Garden. Other speakers and performers included Adam Clayton Powell, newly elected to Congress as the representative from Harlem; Paul Robeson, by then renowned as a singer and actor in both the United States and Europe; and Duke Ellington, jazz composer, performer, and band leader, whom a New Yorker writer had recently dubbed "the hot Bach."

NEGRO FREEDOM RALLY, Madison Square Garden, New York, 1944. Announcement. Prints and Photographs.

(OPPOSITE) **PEARL PRIMUS DANCES "THE NEGRO SPEAKS OF RIVERS,"** photograph by Gerda Petrich, 1944. Mary O'H. Williamson Collection of Colored Celebrities Here and There.

Pearl Primus

TACTICS AND TECHNIQUES. Boycotts, picketing, letter-writing campaigns, sit-ins, the ballot, the press, and marching were just some of the nonviolent means employed by Blacks to protest discrimination in the 1940s and 1950s. At the time, they were called direct action campaigns.

Educator and activist Mary Church Terrell launched a campaign to desegregate public places in Washington, D.C. She had been educated at Oberlin College, receiving a bachelor's degree in 1884—a rare accomplishment for an African-American woman in those times. She became a high school teacher and principal in Washington, D.C., and was appointed to the District's Board of Education. Her husband, Robert Terrell, was a high school principal as well and became the first African-American judge in the District of Columbia's Municipal Court.

In 1950, after Mary Church Terrell and her colleagues were refused service at Thompson's Restaurant, they filed a lawsuit in the District of Columbia. The case took three years to be decided.

In her 80s while the Thompson case was pending, Terrell targeted other public restaurants around Washington that were practicing racial discrimination. She organized boycotts, pickets, and sit-ins to make her point.

In 1953, the court ruled that segregated eating places were unconstitutional. By that time, Mary Church Terrell had turned 90, a figurehead of undaunted persistence in the struggle of Black women for the rights of their people.

MARY CHURCH TERRELL (FOURTH FROM LEFT) PICKETING WITH MEMBERS OF THE COORDINATING COMMITTEE FOR THE ENFORCEMENT OF THE DISTRICT OF COLUMBIA ANTI-DISCRIMINATION LAWS, photographer unknown, ca 1952. Prints and Photographs.

Student Nonviolent
Coordinating Committee

6 Raymond Street, N.W.
Atlanta 14, Georgia

608-0331

Donna Moses
1017 Lynch St.
Jackson Miss.   July 13, 1964

Donna-
The following should arrive via Ryder Truck
Lines, Wednesday, July 15:

13 boxes	(65,000)	Freedom Registration Forms
5 boxes	(25,000)	Freedom registration Brochures
5 boxes	(25,000)	Miss. Freedom Demo Party Brochure
1 box		500 Danger Two Party system Brochure and 2500 Miss. Demo Party Statioary.
1 box	(5,000)	SNCC Newsletter (to be sent to Betty Garmen in Greenwood)
2 boxes		Give Them a Future in Miss. (Panola County) and Mass Meeting (to be sent to Claude Weaver in Batesville - pronto)
27 boxes	Total	via truck to Jackson

    Also Francis Mitchell will carry the following
to Greenwood:

2 boxes	(8,000)	The Independent
1 box		Benefit Dance - Greenwood
1 box	(4,000)	Greenwood Freedom Day Leaflet

4 boxes Total to Greenwood

Please make sure the Panola County stuff gets up
to Claude in Batesville.

Work out,   cc. Betty Garmen
                                       Claude Weaver

Mark Suckle   Julian Bond

LETTER FROM MARK SUCKLE TO DONNA MOSES CONCERNING FREEDOM SUMMER PROJECT (voter registration campaign in Mississippi), July 13, 1964. SNCC, Civil Rights Documentation Project Vertical File.

STUDENT NONVIOLENT COORDINATING COMMITTEE.

The Student Nonviolent Coordinating Committee was started in 1960 in Raleigh, North Carolina, to coordinate nonviolent actions in protest against segregation and racism. Some of SNCC's original members were student organizers of sit-ins at lunch counters throughout the South—planned events during which Black protesters went into segregated restaurants and remained seated, no matter what the restaurant management did or said.

Julian Bond—activist, civil rights historian, and 21st-century chair of the NAACP—was one of the founders of SNCC. He later became the organization's communications director. Bond and other SNCC activists powered voter registration drives in the South, believing that an increase in the number of African-American voters would lead to racial equality. They organized a mock election in Mississippi in 1963. Called the Freedom Ballot, it inspired almost 80,000 Blacks to vote—far more than had been voting in government elections—and showed that the African-American populace had voting power, if they were allowed to wield it. The next summer, called Freedom Summer, SNCC continued efforts to register Black voters in the South.

JULIAN BOND, photographer unknown, ca 1963. SNCC, Civil Rights Documentation Project Vertical File.

VOTER REGISTRATION BUTTON, ca 1963. SNCC, Civil Rights Documentation Project Vertical File.

THE BLACK PANTHERS

WHEN ASKED, I MOST OFTEN TELL curious inquisitors that I joined the Black Panther Party because I had no choice. I was compelled. Most often I still feel that way. I don't know if everyone who became a Panther felt that way, but I know many did. We joined in spite of our first inclination. In the end, the idea of working to educate and liberate the Black community won out.

I found the Black Panther Party after returning from Vietnam, confused by a war that I didn't understand and frustrated by the continuing battle of Black people for civil and human rights. Malcolm was dead, but his call for righteous self-defense was still alive and resonated with me and

other Panthers. For us, self-defense was a logical response to the dogs, the water hoses, the Bull Connors, the killing of little girls in churches, and ultimately the murder of the dreamer, Martin Luther King.

"All power to the people" made sense, as did the party's platform and program, which included a call for land, bread, housing, education, clothing, justice, and peace. So did its rules of discipline and its organization. This was, we thought, an army, fueled by its love for the Black community. I saw this love displayed daily by the young men and women who sold Panther papers and held sway in our community education classes. I was 22, older than most of them by four or five years. Together we were ready to fight, live, and die for the people.

Even in the midst of our attraction we were not unconscious of the dangers that came with membership. The loss of family, incarceration, exile, and death were realities we were living with each day. Someone who was not a member recently told me how much they respected the Panthers, and how heroic we were to stand up for Black people. We never talked—at least I never heard any Panthers talk—about being heroic. We knew Panthers, including Huey and Bobby, were in jails. We also knew Panthers had been murdered, and like Eldridge, many were on the run or had found temporary safety in exile. So while we knew these things, we joined anyway.

So I repeat, it wasn't a question of joining. The question was, how do you resist the chance of setting history right—and at the same time ending all of the injustice heaped on Black people for four centuries plus? We saw it that way, and this was a proposition too compelling and powerful to resist.

I am silent now. Not fully satisfied, my inquisitor continues, "Well, would you do it again?" This question makes me smile. So I ask the inquisitor, "What would you do if you thought you had a chance to set Black people free?" —*W. Paul Coates, former Black Panthers defense captain*

THE BLACK PANTHER NEWSPAPER, vol. 3, no. 2, May 4, 1969. Black Panther Party Papers.

(OPPOSITE) "HERE AND NOW FOR BOBBY SEALE," artist unknown, n.d. Poster. Black Panther Party Papers.

HERE AND NOW FOR BOBBY SEALE

We must save Bobby Seale because
we must save the Black Panther Party because
we must save the revolutionary spirit in America.

THE N.Y. COMMITTEE TO DEFEND THE PANTHERS
NEW HAVEN # 432-8098

Elect

Charles McLaurin and Mrs. Fannie Lou Hamer

S I N C E R E

I N F O R M E D

C A P A B L E

STATE SENATORS
Post No. 1 — Post No. 2
BOLIVAR AND SUNFLOWER COUNTIES

NOVEMBER 2, 1971

THEY WILL BE YOUR VOICE IN THE STATE SENATE FOR THE NEXT FOUR YEARS.

THEY WILL WORK TO:

1. PRESERVE AND UP-GRADE PUBLIC SCHOOLS
2. RAISE TEACHERS' SALARIES
3. REFORM STATE WELFARE AND DISABILITY PROGRAMS
4. ATTRACT MORE AND BETTER INDUSTRY TO THE DISTRICT AND STATE
5. AMEND THE VOTING LAW TO ALLOW STUDENTS, PERSONS IN HOSPITALS AND NURSING HOMES, ETC. TO VOTE BY ABSENTEE BALLOTS
6. ESTABLISH COMPULSORY SCHOOL ATTENDANCE LAW
7. ENACT A STATEWIDE PUBLIC HOUSING LAW

VOTE FOR PROGRESS NOV. 2

GETTING OUT THE VOTE. Throughout the 1960s, the force and significance of distinctions based on race and class became more apparent in the light of continuing protests and social upheaval. Uprisings exploded in Cleveland, Detroit, Watts in Los Angeles, Harlem in New York, and other cities across the nation. Protests against racial inequality connected with national demonstrations against the Vietnam War and international struggles against imperialism.

Among civil rights activists, one of the most important campaigns waged during this decade was the demand for equal voting rights for all citizens of the U.S. Although the Constitution's 15th Amendment had guaranteed the right the vote for all, local governments still employed a number of methods that had the effect of preventing African Americans from casting their ballots at the polls.

In August 1965 President Lyndon B. Johnson signed into effect the Voting Rights Act of 1965, which went further to enforce the right to vote and opened the door for the advancement of Black political power.

CAMPAIGN BUTTONS *(CLOCKWISE)*: Eldridge Cleaver for President, Peace and Freedom Party, 1968; Dick Gregory for President, Peace and Freedom Party, 1968; and Hope, Future, Peace in Watts, California, ca 1965. Button Collection, Howard University Museum.

(OPPOSITE) **"ELECT CHARLES MCLAURIN AND MRS. FANNIE LOU HAMER,"** Mississippi, 1971. Poster. Civil Rights Documentation Project Vertical File.

THE MARCH ON WASHINGTON. On August 28, 1963, a quarter of a million people gathered in the nation's capital for a crowning event in the history of race relations in the United States. Planners called it the March on Washington for Jobs and Freedom, but it has gone down in history as simply "The March on Washington." It is remembered as the occasion on which Martin Luther King, Jr., delivered his momentous speech, "I Have a Dream."

The 1963 March on Washington had its roots in the 1941 march planned by A. Philip Randolph, president of the Brotherhood of Sleeping Car Porters, to demand jobs for Blacks during wartime.

In 1962, Randolph and other civil rights leaders, including Martin Luther King, began discussion about a large demonstration in the nation's capital that would bring attention to inequities and the need for jobs for Black Americans.

On the 20th anniversary of the 1963 event, March on Washington II celebrated America's continued commitment to justice and equality for all Americans.

"I'M FOR NATIONAL KING DAY," 1985. Denim/Velcro armband. Omnium Gatherum Collection.

BANNER AND BUTTONS FROM THE MARCH ON WASHINGTON II, 1983. General Museum Collection.

(OPPOSITE) **"JOBS, PEACE, FREEDOM,"** 1983. Poster for March on Washington II. Prints and Photographs.

20th Anniversary of the Historic 1963 March on Washington

JOBS PEACE FREEDOM

August 27, 1983 ☆ Lincoln Memorial ☆ Washington, D.C.

ASSEMBLY POINT:

Marchers will assemble at 8:00 a.m. on the Mall, bordered by 14th and 3rd Streets, N.W. The Mall is located directly between the Washington Monument and the U.S. Capitol. An inspirational program will feature artists/entertainers/selected speakers which will begin at 9:00 a.m. The actual March to the Lincoln Memorial will start 10:30 a.m.

MARCH ROUTE:

The March will begin on 14th Street at the Mall, proceeding north to Constitution Avenue, west on Constitution to 17th, and south on 17th to feed into the Lincoln Memorial grounds at the Reflecting Pool.

PROGRAM:

The program for the March will begin at 1:00 p.m. at the Lincoln Memorial. At that time, major speeches on the theme of Jobs, Peace and Freedom will be delivered.

For More Information, Call or Write:

MARCH ON WASHINGTON
1201 16th Street, N.W.
Suite 219
Washington, D.C.
(202) 467-6445 or 1-800-638-6415

LOCAL CONTACT:

CHAPTER 11

The Black Arts Movement

1960s-1970s

The Black Art Movement was realized by members of the art faculty at H.U. Prof. James Wells, James Porter and I. We were pioneers in introducing the movement among our students, Eliz. Catlett, Malkia, Delilah Pierce and others.

With the assassination of Martin Luther King the Black Art Movement launched on an intensified momentum which resulted in nationwide presentations of "Black Art Shows."

Black artists were determined to establish their identity and to offer to the black community an art which reflected customs, traditions and the beauty of black people.

Lois Mailou Jones, n.d.
Class notes on the Black Arts Movement

1960s-1970s *The Harlem-based Black Arts Movement (BAM) placed an emphasis on the importance of culture to the liberation struggle and stimulated a Black consciousness in the arts. Sometimes considered the Second Black Renaissance, BAM began around 1964, when circles of writers, artists, and activists began discussions about the need for a new Black aesthetic that would not just embrace the "Black Is Beautiful" accolade but would encompass pride in the legacy of Black achievement throughout the diaspora. Students on Black campuses argued for a more Afrocentric curriculum across disciplines. Conferences and annual symposiums examined Black themes and enhanced new academic programs. The first National Black Arts Festival was held in Detroit in 1966.*

Artistic expression led to a psychological connection with Africa. For example, artist Lois Mailou Jones incorporated the colors and patterns of African textiles and sculpture in her paintings. Unlike the Black Renaissance of the early 20th century, in which Black artistic traditions emulated those of Europeans, the new Black artists of the 1970s felt free to create and define a Black aesthetic and to explore the genres of film, the performing and visual arts, and literature.

HOWARD UNIVERSITY AND THE BLACK ARTS MOVEMENT

THE BLACK ARTS MOVEMENT (BAM)—also known as the New Black Renaissance or the Second Black Renaissance—exploded on the scene sometime during the mid-1960s from sparks that flew out from the double fiery infernos known as the civil rights and Black power movements. Regarded by Larry Neal, one of the movement's chief critics and architects, as the "spiritual sister of the Black Power concept," this massive Black cultural awakening rallied Black artists in efforts to shape a "separate symbolism, mythology, critique, and iconology." The chief raison d'être of this popular movement was to reject and subvert the Western aesthetic. The new Black aesthetic inspired spirituals, gospels, blues and jazz rhythms, poetry, dance, and theater. It not only showcased an abundance of creative genius among African Americans but also conveyed a united front, using art as instruments—or weapons—of revolution.

The Black Arts Movement had no permanent address. Avoiding similar misconceptions that surrounded the Harlem Renaissance about place of origin, BAM does not claim any one city or any one institution as its home base; the movement seemed too large to be contained and centrally located. At the height of BAM, from 1965 to 1976, virtually every African-American community and many college campuses across America saw a significant rise in the number of new Black theaters and arts organizations that plugged their programs into a decidedly Black cultural nationalist agenda.

"MOON MASQUE," by Lois Mailou Jones, 1971. Note card of original painting. Lois Mailou Jones Papers.

At the height of the Black Arts Movement, many of its advocates petitioned, picketed, and parlayed to establish African-American studies programs on college campuses. In the mid-1960s, Howard University's own Afro-American Studies Department emerged. Local and national headlines reflected the passion that Howard's own students had in favor of shifting the frame of reference for their studies from European works to those written by African Americans and other writers of the African diaspora: *Negro Digest* printed an article about "The Black Power Rebellion at Howard University" in December 1967, and *Jet* reported "Students Take Over Howard University, Want Black University Concept" in April 1968. Staging sit-ins, forming human chains to block access, holding mass rallies, and boycotting classes were just a few of the strategies used by a younger generation bent on permanently changing the curriculum at Howard. The students stood their ground and were successful in implementing a Black course of study and a department that has flourished and achieved national renown since then.

Howard students did not wage this campaign alone. A significant segment of its faculty was just as passionately involved in pressuring the institution to lead the way among the nation's major institutions in emphasizing literary and cultural studies in the African diaspora. Most influential in directing his energy and intellect to this cause was literary critic, author, and educator Stephen Henderson, who served as the English Department chair from 1962 to 1971. In 1971 Henderson joined the Afro-American Studies Department, where he set about building institutions buoyed by his belief that the BAM "attempts to speak directly to Black people about themselves in order to move them toward self-knowledge and collective freedom. Much of the work produced at this time is considered art of liberating vision: liberation from slavery, from segregation and degradation, from wishful 'integration' into the 'mainstream,' to the passionate denial of white middle-class values of the present and an attendant embrace of Africa and the third world as alternative routes of development." Henderson's most significant literary contribution is his *Understanding the New Black Poetry: Black Speech and Black Music as Poetic References* (1973), in which he offers a new framework for literary criticism, dialogue, and debate among writers attempting to synthesize the social, political, and cultural issues of the BAM period.

In the late 1960s and early 1970s, Henderson was part of an initiative among major universities to create cultural studies centers to address social issues and bridge the academic and public communities. He led such an effort at Howard University under the aegis of an organization known as the Institute for Arts and Humanities (1973-86), whose primary mission was to support scholarship on African-American culture. This institute quickly became a think tank that attracted artist-activists such as Andrew Billingsley, John O. Killens, Haki Madhubuti, and Sterling A. Brown. The group agreed to support the documentation and preservation of work by artists, scholars, and intellectuals of color, and it encouraged new productions, thus linking a significant portion of the inheritance of the Black Arts Movement to Washington, D.C., and Howard University. As a result of Henderson's groundbreaking scholarship and activism, he earned the university a prominent place among institutions sharing the mission to preserve Black culture and continue to affirm the importance of Black cultural identity.

Today, college campuses throughout the nation still bear testimony to the lasting impact of the Black Arts Movement. African-American studies departments arose in response to the movement's push to infuse a new Black aesthetic that rescued the African-American experience from the margins by putting the work of writers such as Margaret Walker, Richard Wright, James Baldwin, Robert Hayden, Ernest Gaines, and Gwendolyn Brooks in the foreground. Through it all, Howard University has been a vital link. At one time or another, several of the movement's leading writers, artists, and activists matriculated there. Some received degrees; some taught; others found themselves at odds with Howard's administration and had their university stays terminated prematurely. One such figure, Amiri Baraka—poet, playwright, and activist—never completed his degree, but today he continues to be a key link between the movement and the university.

Affectionately—and perhaps rather generously—known as the father of the Black Arts Movement, Baraka was born LeRoi Jones. He changed his name in 1967, in the wake of Malcolm X's 1965 assassination. His poem "Black Art," written during that same time, quickly became the major poetic manifesto of the Black Arts Movement. "We want poems that kill," Jones declared in "Black Art." He was not simply speaking metaphorically. His most popular plays, the critically acclaimed *Dutchman* and *The Slave*, stopped short of calling for outright physical violence against white oppression but advocated artistic and political freedom "by any means necessary."

LeRoi Jones transferred to Howard University from Rutgers in 1952. Two years later, it is written, he "flunked out of Howard" and enlisted in the U.S. Air Force. During his tenure as a Howard student, he was a constant vocal critic of the university administration's policies, which often stood in opposition to BAM's principles. He often took the position that the Howard experience catered more to the bourgeoisie or the upper class. His autobiography records a familiar episode, when he purposely and tauntingly sat on the steps of Howard's administration building eating a slice of watermelon, bringing to mind the darky stereotype made popular by the likes of plantation school writers Joel Chandler Harris and Thomas Nelson Page.

Despite his turbulent relationship with the university, Amiri Baraka has donated his papers to the Moorland-Spingarn Research Center for safekeeping and research. His influence seemed tangential while he was a student at Howard, but now history records him as the dominant figure in the movement. Larry Neal, an essayist, poet, critic, and author of the 1968 manifesto "The Black Arts Movement," wrote: "In drama, LeRoi Jones represents the most advanced aspects of the movement. He is its prime mover and chief designer.... The Black Arts theatre, the theatre of LeRoi Jones, is a radical alternative to the sterility of the American theatre. It is primarily a theatre of the Spirit, confronting the Black Man in his interaction with his brothers and with the white thing."

The link between Amiri Baraka, Howard University, and the Moorland-Spingarn Research Center is now unbreakable. Still intensely outspoken and committed as a writer, Baraka will inevitably continue to be examined for his ongoing efforts to celebrate and argue the case for Blackness in all of its various forms. It is fitting that the Moorland-Spingarn Research Center at Howard now represents a prime research site to visit to explore all that went into Stephen Henderson's and Amiri Baraka's passionate and committed efforts to use Black arts as a means to advocate, to educate, and to remember. —*Sandra G. Shannon, Howard University*

I

The New Negro Movement
or Harlem Renaissance
or
The Negro Renaissance ESTABLISHED
~~which~~ emerged in the
1920's in Harlem
→ where [For the 1st time in
American History the black
intellectuals - Artists,
writers, poets and scholars
joined the musicians in
documenting a positive
sense of identity as related
to their black heritage.

In MUSIC singers such as
Bessie Smith
Fats Waller
Billie Holiday
Louis Armstrong ←
(Afro Cobra)
In Literature writers : Sam Gilliam
Claude McKay · Romare
James Weldon Johnson ·Bearden
Countee Cullen Hughie
Langston Hughes Lee
In Visual Arts - Painters: ~~Aaron~~ Smith
Meta Warrick
Fuller
· Augusta Savage ✗ Aaron Douglas ✗ ↑
Gwen Bennett Archibald Motley
Sargent Johnson
Influence of. Palmer Hayden
Winold Reiss, Wm H. Johnson
(austrian)
Sculptor: Richmond James Wells
Barthé Hale Woodruff
Joined in documenting a positive
sense of identity as related to their
black heritage. Paying tribute to their
African heritage

THE VISUAL ARTS. In the October 1926 issue of *Crisis*, W. E. B. Du Bois wrote a response to a survey of the ways in which Black people had been portrayed in the arts. "All art is propaganda and ever must be," Du Bois stated.

Likewise the visual artist of the Black Arts Movement of the 1960s rejected the school of thought that valued art for art's sake. Instead, many artists aligned themselves with the Black power movement, believing that the purpose of their art was to teach and uplift Black people and to strengthen their sense of empowerment.

In this time of heightened racial consciousness, theories about art and identity were heavily debated. A sense of the importance of art was evident, and a respect for the influences coming from all that had been created by Black artists past and present, as shown in the notes made by Lois Mailou Jones for her Howard University classes.

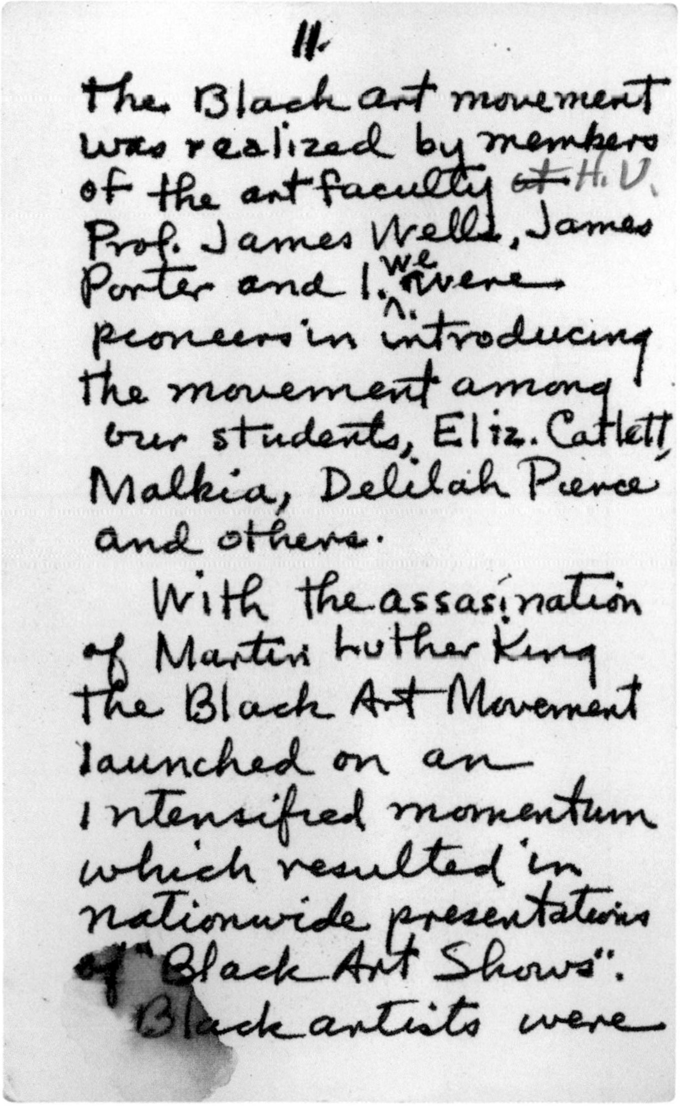

11.

The Black art movement was realized by members of the art faculty at H.U. Prof. James Wells, James Porter and I. we were pioneers in introducing the movement among our students, Eliz. Catlett, Malkia, Delilah Pierce and others.

With the assasination of Martin Luther King the Black Art Movement launched on an intensified momentum which resulted in nationwide presentations of "Black Art Shows". Black artists were

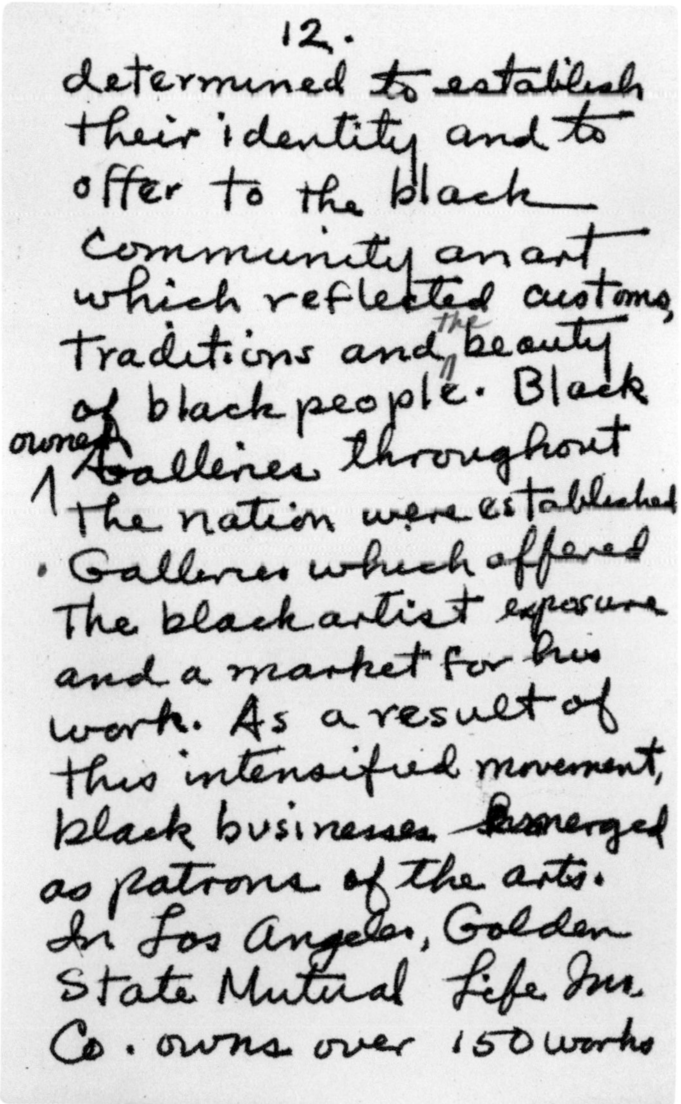

12.

determined to establish their identity and to offer to the black community an art which reflected customs, traditions and the beauty of black people. Black owned Galleries throughout the nation were established. Galleries which offered the black artist exposure and a market for his work. As a result of this intensified movement, black businesses emerged as patrons of the arts. In Los Angeles, Golden State Mutual Life Ins. Co. owns over 150 works

CLASS NOTES ON THE BLACK ART MOVEMENT, pages 11 and 12, Lois Mailou Jones, n.d. Lois Mailou Jones Papers.

(OPPOSITE) **CLASS NOTES ON THE NEW NEGRO MOVEMENT OR HARLEM RENAISSANCE,** Lois Mailou Jones, n.d. Lois Mailou Jones Papers.

AMIRI BARAKA. A politically active artist and one of the most influential writers of the Black Arts Movement, Amiri Baraka was born Everett Leroy Jones in Newark, New Jersey, in 1934. He changed his name to LeRoi Jones while studying literature under Sterling Brown at Howard University in the 1950s, then in 1967 he adopted the Arabic name Imamu Amiri Baraka.

Baraka began as a beat poet in Greenwich Village. Two of his most influential works appeared in 1963: *Blues People: Negro Music in White America*, a cultural history, and *Dutchman*,

a play that premiered in New York in 1964 and won an Obie Award as the year's best off-Broadway play.

Soon after, Baraka catapulted out of the beat scene and into the vibrant arts world of Harlem. He restaged *Dutchman* in Harlem, presenting it to the Black audience for whom he had written it. In May 1965 he opened the Black Arts Repertory Theatre School (BART), which offered courses on African-American culture and history, music, and dance, setting the standard for all Black studies programs that followed.

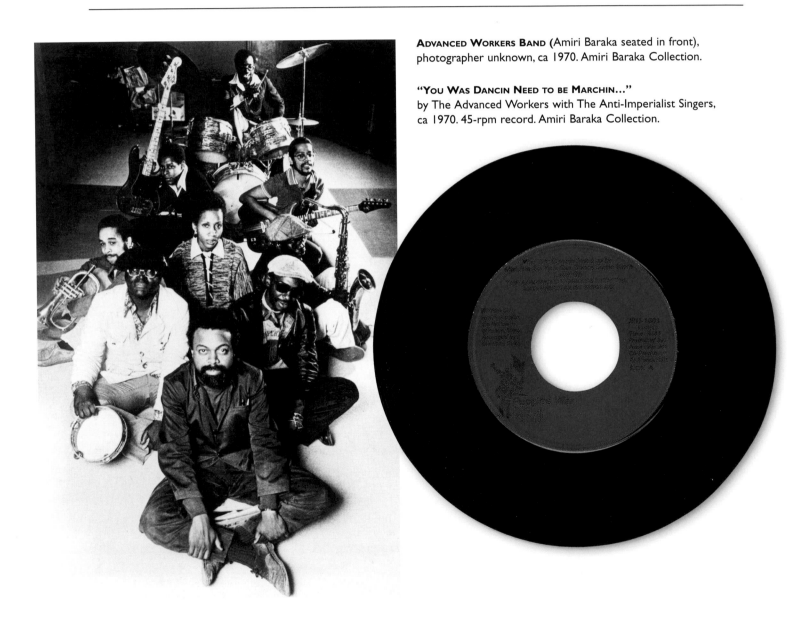

ADVANCED WORKERS BAND (Amiri Baraka seated in front), photographer unknown, ca 1970. Amiri Baraka Collection.

"YOU WAS DANCIN NEED TO BE MARCHIN..."
by The Advanced Workers with The Anti-Imperialist Singers, ca 1970. 45-rpm record. Amiri Baraka Collection.

(OPPOSITE) **"THE BLACK ARTS REPERTORY THEATRE SCHOOL,"** ca 1965. Poster. Amiri Baraka Collection.

THE BLACK ARTS
REPERTORY THEATRE SCHOOL
109 W. 130TH STREET, NEW YORK 10027

poem

of

angela yvonne davis

by
nikki giovanni

C. GLENN CARRINGTON, COLLECTOR. While attending Howard University, Calvin Glenn Carrington developed a love for books. Through association with key figures of the Black Renaissance—including Alain Locke, Georgia Douglass Johnson, and Langston Hughes—Carrington acquired important artifacts of the Black experience. Soon he became an avid collector of material central to the documentation of modern Black American history.

Carrington's collection represents 50 years of documentation. It contains precious and fascinating pieces from the period of the Black Renaissance of the 1920s through the Black Arts Movement of the 1970s. Among the treasures of the C. Glenn Carrington Collection are autographed first editions of books, programs from landmark performances, photographs, recordings, broadsides, and sheet music. The total represents a comprehensive documentary of Black visual, literary, and performing artistry and supports the claim of Black Arts Movement thinkers that artists create their work for the larger public out of a sense of social responsibility.

(LEFT) **JACOB LAWRENCE,** photograph by Glenn Carrington, n.d. C. Glenn Carrington Collection.

(RIGHT) **DUKE ELLINGTON,** photographer unknown, 1970. Program of NAACP benefit gala, Madison Square Garden, February 29. Autographed by B.B. King, Eubie Blake, Nobel Sissle, and others. C. Glenn Carrington Collection.

(OPPOSITE) **"POEM OF ANGELA YVONNE DAVIS,"** by Nikki Giovanni, autographed to Glenn Carrington on February 28, 1972. C. Glenn Carrington Collection.

THE SPACE IN BETWEEN: RESEARCH AND ADVOCACY

PHOTOGRAPHY IS THE SPACE IN BETWEEN—that space where I find my voice as a photographer and writer about African-American photographic practices. The invitation to contribute to this volume came when I was writing about the significance of portraiture in African-American visual culture. I started to write about photography as a cultural research tool and about the collection at the Moorland-Spingarn Research Center (MSRC) as an archive of activist photography because I think the collections offer a view of African-American life different from that found

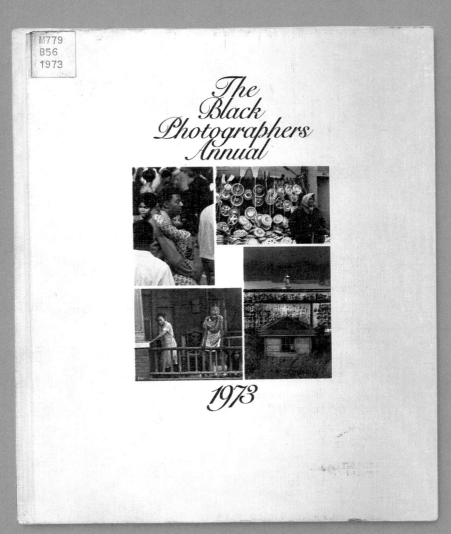

in other repositories. There is an understanding of the importance of visual culture as another storytelling device. The center remains a central place for photography for families who consider their own photo collections as historical documents as well as for photographers looking for a home to preserve their life's work. As historian Robin D. G. Kelley states, "In a world where the deliberate distortion of black images in popular culture was as common as ice vendors in turn-of-the-century cities in August, the camera became a mighty weapon in the hands of pioneering black photographers."

As I began to consider these issues, however, a different story began to emerge—one that was highly personal and incorporated within the collective voice of Black artists. In the 1960s and 1970s, Black artists created work in response to activities related to

the civil rights movement. Living in the cities of Washington, Philadelphia, Atlanta, New York, Chicago, Los Angeles, and Oakland, they formed the collaborative that became known as the Black Arts Movement.

(ABOVE) *THE BLACK PHOTOGRAPHERS ANNUAL 1973,* by Joe Crawford, New York, 1972. Library Collection.

(OPPOSITE) *THE TRADITION CONTINUES: CALIFORNIA BLACK PHOTOGRAPHERS,* by California Museum of Afro-American History and Culture, Los Angeles, 1983. Exhibit catalog. Library Collection.

I was one of many inspired by these Black photographers and artists who documented, questioned, and reinterpreted the events that had created the perception of the so-called American experience. My central quest at that time was to use the MSRC collection to create a broader history of American photography. I sought to expand the popular visual historical documents to include works that identified African Americans as image-makers as well as subjects. I saw myself as part of the tradition of artists and scholars who were motivated to present a more inclusive history of American culture.

In this prestigious collection I saw images of musicians, visual and performing artists, political leaders, writers, and activists that I knew could create a revised history of American visual culture. I saw portraits of activist artists, raising their fists with the Black power sign, documenting meetings, hairstyles, and clothing—T-shirts, leather jackets, and dashikis. There were portraits of artists such as Paul Robeson, Bernice Johnson Reagon, and Marvin Gaye, who sang protest songs to voice their displeasure with the plight of Black Americans. Represented in the collection were works by photographers like Maurice Sorrell, Sharon Farmer, Griffith J. Davis, Robert H. McNeill, Robert and George Scurlock, Roland Freeman, Roy Lewis, and David "Oggi" Ogburn. They were witnesses who forged a link between the viewer and the event. They were the historians who documented social protests and community activism. They were the artists who created portraits of a distinct and complex community.

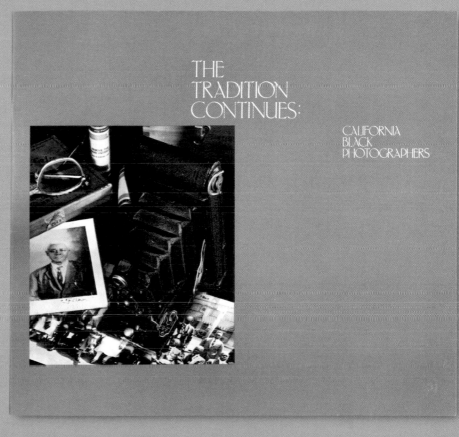

The photograph collection at the MSRC forms a unique visual record of experiences of African Americans during the Black Arts Movement. The collection gives a way to enter the past and learn about the societal issues that have shaped not only our visual culture but, in many ways, the American culture we know today. The MSRC collection was an instrumental part of my research; for many others, it has had an equally formative and inspirational influence. Thanks to Moorland Spingarn, many of us have been able to read, touch, visualize, and perhaps create a more accurate history of the American experience. —*Deborah Willis, New York University*

MELVIN DEAL DANCERS. Historically, music and dance have played an important role in the life of African peoples in their original homeland and throughout the diaspora. These art forms play key roles in worship and celebrations of birth, marriage, and harvest and still thrive on the energy of their ancient roots.

The African Heritage Dancers and Drummers originated in the Shaw area of Washington, D.C., in 1960 as part of a Black cultural awareness program. The group was one of the first Black performing arts projects in the District. Following in the tradition of dancers Katherine Dunham and Pearl Primus, founder Melvin Deal is a cultural anthropologist who traveled to Africa frequently and extensively, studying music, dance, and drumming with African master artists in order to energize and authenticate his work.

MELVIN DEAL PERFORMERS AT THE NATIONAL CONFERENCE OF AFRO-AMERICAN WRITERS, photograph by Roy Lewis, ca 1974. National Conference of Afro-American Writers Photograph Collection.

CHAPTER 12
Leadership
1970s-

Britain did not volunteer to free the thirteen colonies. We fought for freedom. America did not volunteer to free the slaves. Abolition came as a war measure designed to help win the war and thereby save the Union. England did not voluntarily give India her freedom. Hundreds of thousands of Indians went to jail for freedom. Nehru and Gandhi were literally jail birds. The African nations gained their freedom through sweat, blood, and tears. Civil Rights are coming to Negroes in America through Supreme Court pressure, legislation, the wise use of the ballot, boycotts, or some other form of pressure. So the role of the leader is to know the nature of man and understand the events of history so that whatever program of action he projects it will be based on reality.

Benjamin Mays, 1965
Speech, "The Role of Leadership
in a Time of Crisis"

Presented to

The Howard University

From the National Aeronautics and
Space Administration

Frederick Drew Gregory
Pilot, STS 51-B

This flag and crew patch were flown
during the Spacelab 3 Mission

1970s-

The Roman god Janus, patron of the beginning and the end, is portrayed with two faces peering in opposite directions. A similar West African sculpture depicts a deity with the powers to see both the past and the future at the same time. Collecting and preserving the past for future study can be personified in the same way.

A history of leadership, regardless of the field or the level, is one of the most precious components of any legacy left to future generations. The key is in channeling that history into future leaders through interpretation and guidance. The files, publications, and printed matter generated by organizations founded while American society was segregated not only document the role of Black women and men in politics, entertainment, economics, religion, education, and other fields, but also demonstrate how collective power can force change. The oral histories, autobiographies, and personal papers left by entrepreneurs, ministers, lawyers, and educators contribute to our understanding of leadership at the grassroots level and in more prominent roles. They also serve as templates for leaders in the making. By preserving this legacy, future generations can learn and grow, then pass on their knowledge and wisdom to the next.

CHALLENGES OF BLACK LEADERSHIP IN THE 21ST CENTURY

SINCE THE CIVIL RIGHTS MOVEMENT BEGAN in the 1830s and the first Black elected officials took their seats in the 1870s, Black leaders have had two exceedingly difficult mandates: to move effectively in their own communities and to represent the interests of their community in the larger society. Into the 21st century Black leaders have served their own community through such organizations as the National Association for the Advancement of Colored People (NAACP), the National Urban League, the Rainbow/PUSH Coalition, the National Action Network, and the Southern Christian Leadership Conference. Inspired by such organizations, the Voting Rights Act of 1965 set the stage for the arrival of a new wave of elected officials, and the number of Black women and men elected to public office in the United States reached nearly 10,000 by the early 21st century.

In the past three decades, ironically, the new wave of Black elected officials at local levels has occurred during the emergence of a more conservative national political culture, which posed a powerful counterforce, altered the flow of funds for urban economic development, and changed the relationship of government to the less fortunate. Mainstream Black political and religious leaders have responded by publicly rejecting tax cuts for the wealthy, opposing the war in Iraq, fighting against budget reductions in the social sector, and rejecting other regressive aspects of public policy.

FLAG AND PATCH OF COL. FREDERICK DREW GREGORY, PILOT OF SPACE SHUTTLE STS-51B/SPACELAB 3. The first Black to pilot a spacecraft, Gregory flew on April 29, 1985, and carried into space the Spingarn Medal that had been awarded to his uncle, Dr. Charles R. Drew, in 1944. Charles R. Drew Collection, Howard University Museum.

A major focal point for their efforts was the arrival of Hurricane Katrina on the Gulf Coast in August 2005, in response to which the Congressional Black Caucus (CBC) quickly fashioned a package of legislative proposals. Black leaders headed demonstrations in New Orleans, Baton Rouge, and other places to call attention to what they saw as the lack of an effective national response to the devastation. Black leaders met with President George W. Bush the following December and received assurances that their concerns would be taken into consideration on matters related to Katrina, reauthorization of the Voting Rights Act, and the budget. Although they emerged with confidence, the administration later rejected the proposed $30 billion spending package for Katrina as excessive and failed to incorporate the Congressional Black Caucus's proposals into the State of the Union Address.

Black civil rights and political leaders alike have visibly opposed tactics of voter disenfranchisement, especially in Florida in 2000 and Ohio in 2004. In those elections Blacks and other citizens experienced difficulty in casting their votes, faced with fewer polling stations and missing ballot boxes in Black neighborhoods; polling locations shifted without notice; individuals excluded from voter rolls or misidentified as felons; inaccurate voting instructions; problematic voting equipment; and the closure of voting stations with people waiting to vote. In 2001 African-American leaders—including politician and former head of the NAACP Kweisi Mfume and Mary Berry, a former assistant secretary of education and chairwoman of the U.S. Civil Rights Commission—spoke out against voter interference. In 2004, Congressman John Conyers, Jr., of Michigan, a founding member of the CBC, led investigations into the voting practices that occurred in Ohio.

FOLLOWING THE EXAMPLE OF REV. JESSE JACKSON, Sr., two Black presidential candidates, Rev. Al Sharpton of New York and former Senator Carol Moseley Braun of Chicago, entered the 2004 race. The time was not conducive to a Black candidacy, however, because of the tremendous opposition to the Iraq war and the desire of Democratic voters for a nominee who could compete effectively with a sitting Republican President.

Thus, John Kerry of Massachusetts, a former Vietnam War hero, garnered most of the Black votes in the Democratic primary, reducing the opportunity to exercise the leverage of the Black vote. Meanwhile the Black vote for George W. Bush doubled, from 9 percent in 2000 to 18 percent in 2004, with even more significant increases in some states. Most analysts attributed this increase to the appeal of moral stands, such as opposition to gay marriage. Black religious leaders appear to have elevated their concern over such moral issues, which have little direct impact on the quality of life of their parishioners, over more basic issues such as employment, education, and health, which do have direct impact and are the primary responsibility of political institutions. The conservative political movement attracted some Black religious leaders, such as Bishop Harry Jackson, Jr., leader of Hope Christian Church in Lanham, Maryland, who heads a small but politically visible group of Black conservatives who have been dependable supporters of the Bush Administration's policies.

But behind dedicated Black political conservatives, however, is a maturing emphasis on economic spiritualism in the growth of Black churches into "megachurches," substantial institutions serving thousands of people with an array of funded service projects. Illustrative of this trend is The Potter's House, a church institution in Dallas headed by Rev. T. D. Jakes, with a membership of 30,000, a staff of more than 400, and a service outreach of more than 50 ministries. Some are reluctant to continue the legacy of considering the Black church as the base for political mobilization for social justice causes, not only to avoid the politicization of moral issues but also because churches risk losing the benefit of the Bush Administration's faith-based funding for social services. At the other extreme, though, Minister Louis Farrakhan drew more than 500,000 people to the Millions More Movement, commemorating the tenth anniversary of the October 1995 Million Man March.

AT THIS WRITING, the conservative movement is dominant in the White House, the House, the Senate, and state governorships. The elevation of John Roberts and Samuel Alito to the Supreme Court may seriously tilt future Court decisions in the same direction as well. Extensive research by the Alliance for Justice has shown that Alito has tended in most cases to oppose civil rights complaints, siding with employers against workers, and to believe that the decision the Court reached in *Roe* v. *Wade* was wrong.

These trends may place greater pressure on Black leaders to shift strategies, use more effective campaign tactics and civic participation, and emphasize changing the complexion of Congress and state legislatures. Black civic organizations may be called upon to play a greater role in providing both financial and organizational resources, such as those found in the National Coalition on Black Civic Participation, dedicated to voter mobilization. Political participation will require greater attention to financial contributions, agenda setting, community mobilization, message development, and candidate selection at all levels. The focus of opportunity for electing Black candidates and those sympathetic to Black interests should shift to statewide office at both the state and federal level. Some evidence of this shift already exists, with the election of Illinois state Senator Barack Obama to the U.S. Senate and the national attention he is attracting as a political leader.

Although the effectiveness of Black leaders can lead to positive results, the sphere of their authority is severely limited. In fact, white leaders have had much more to do with the quality of life than Black leaders, and as such have become the primary targets for either supportive coalitions or pressure for change. The existing cadre of Black leaders must seek additional power with greater creativity and exploit all opportunities. In light of the challenge of a political system likely to pose significant challenges to the Black community, there is a need for more urgent attention to strengthening the infrastructure of Black leaders and their organizations to create pressure and formulate cooperative measures for social change. In that task, leaders will need to retain the defiant spirit and tactics of the civil rights movement. —*Ronald Walters, University of Maryland*

Responsibility

Official Organ

The National Association of Negro Business and Professional Women's Clubs, Inc.

The chains around the world are breaking gradually—
and—total freedom arising—in the horizon

Anna Land Butler

Price— .50c

BUSINESS AND ENTREPRENEURSHIP. Archives from professional clubs and associations offer rich collections of information on Black people and how they have participated in a variety of disciplines and professions.

These collections are the record of their own history, and they can serve their organizations as well as those outside by encouraging continuity in future goals, programs, initiatives, and leadership. Designated sections of the archives of the Alpha Kappa Alpha Sorority, Inc., for

example, are consulted yearly by potential pledges, who are called on to familiarize themselves with the sorority's programs of the past.

Founded in 1935, the National Association of Negro Business and Professional Women's Clubs, Inc., continues to be a leader in international cooperation in business and assists in developing programs for women and children. The archives of its decades of planning, work, and leadership provide inspiration to many.

UNITED NATIONS REPRESENTATIVE DAISY GEORGE TALKS WITH VILLAGERS IN NAIROBI, photographer unknown, 1977. NANBPWC Papers.

(OPPOSITE) RESPONSIBILITY, The National Association of Negro Business and Professional Women's Clubs, Inc., Washington, D.C., vol. XIV, no. 2, Fall 1957. NANBPWC Papers.

THE FIELD OF BLACK STUDIES

BLACK STUDIES EMERGED as a discipline through the integration of community activism and scholarship, resulting in a field centered on the experiences and history of people of African descent in the United States and the diaspora. The main challenge of Black studies is to right wrongheaded depictions of African-American life and culture in the United States through the exploration of African-American life and history throughout the diaspora.

Black studies programs and departments were institutionalized in the late 1960s and the 1970s, mirroring the social and political climate of the time and laying the foundation for the activist-scholar

paradigm. The investigation of Black folk, however, began long before the ivory tower incorporated Black studies departments. The first three generations of scholarship in and public acknowledgment of Black life and culture appeared in publications that highlighted the contributions and explained the conditions of Black life in the United States. A few works made the connection to a glorious African past. A small network of Black scholars began disrupting acceptable depictions of Black family, civic, and social life with their accurate research into Black life and culture. Today, exploring the interconnectedness of people of African descent constitutes a mainstream area of study.

Another major theme of Black studies in the past 25 years has been Black women's studies, which is a program within the Black studies program at a few universities and colleges. Black women's studies explores gender politics, religious expression and experience, feminist theory and practice, sexuality, representations of Black women in popular culture, and activist practices and how they are articulated and integrated in Black experiences.

The third major area and point of growth in Black studies is the examination of institutions and organizations centered in Black community life, such as various church denominations and historical and social groups like Black fraternities and sororities.

Born out of political movements to correct depictions of Black people, Black studies is an ever evolving discipline, one that enriches both scholarship and activism. Black studies is not made up solely of academic disciplines locked in an ivory tower. There is an ebb and flow between the public and the academic, and that connection will continue to be essential to Black studies. Understanding how experiences of people of African descent interface with all types of human institutions and conditions is the ongoing mission of all who pursue Black studies. —*Deidre Hill Butler, Union College*

PEARL PRIMUS IN *VOGUE,* August 1, 1943. Mary O'H. Williamson Collection of Colored Celebrities Here and There.

(*OPPOSITE*) **COLORED AVIATORS IN** *FLASH* **MAGAZINE,** April 5, 1938. Mary O'H. Williamson Collection of Colored Celebrities Here and There.

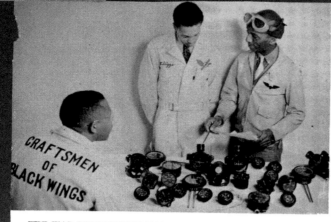

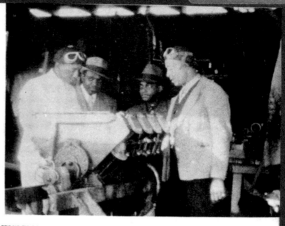

THE WAR DEPARTMENT HAS AIDED this aviation group by furnishing over $800 worth of airplane instruments for class instruction.

MUSICIANS REX STEWART AND HAYES ALVIS are seen as they visited the humming Craftmen's engine shops.

COLORED AIR CIRCUS

"FIVE BLACKBIRDS" - ONLY COLORED AVIATORS

COL. RUPERT JULIAN | MABE DAUGHTRY - CHUTE JUMPER | MATTHEW J. CHAMPARA
WORLD FAMOUS COLORED AVIATOR | MARIE DICKERSON AVIATRIX | - The Human Arrow

FRANK SEBASTIAN'S COTTON CLUB ORCHESTRA & ENTERTAINERS

LOS ANGELES EASTSIDE AIRPORT
800 EAST WHITTIER BLVD. - ½ MILE EAST OF MONTEBELLO

SUNDAY - DECEMBER 6TH

15,000 HAVE WITNESSED CRAFTSMEN SHOWS. True to the spirit of the State, push is given the project.

THEY KNOW THEIR AIRLANES AND AIRPLANES. William Aikens, William Johnson, Marie Dickerson and Irvin Wells are pictured

DOCUMENTING BLACKS AND RECREATION.

To provide documentation on recreational disciplines, archival initiatives in dance, skating, and golf began at Moorland. These are examples of initiatives sure to help preserve the stories of underrepresented aspects of Black history.

Recreational histories are grounded in community self-help programs that were started by individuals and organizations banned from mainstream facilities, both private and public.

As an example, Our Family Skate Association, part of the National African American Roller Skating Archives Project, continues its 20-year mission to educate the general public about the health and social benefits of roller skating and its unique history within the Black community.

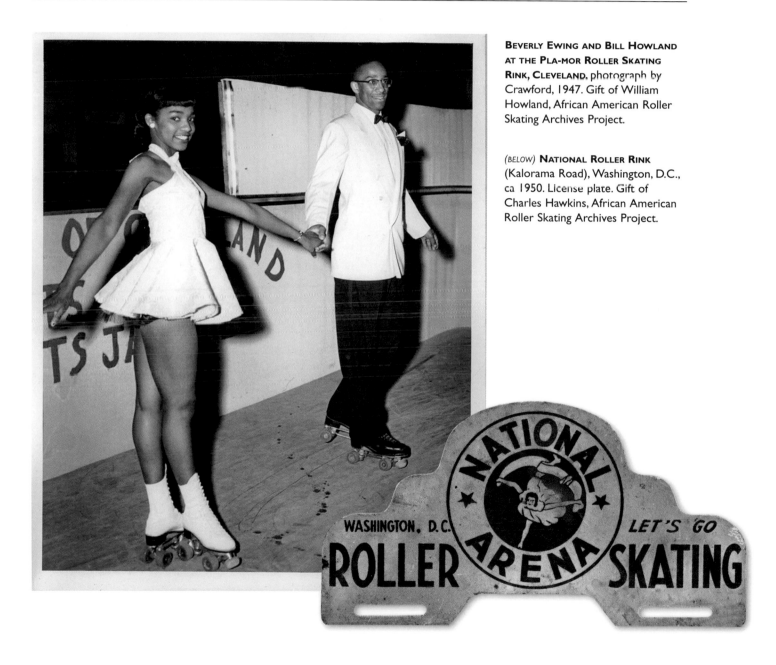

BEVERLY EWING AND BILL HOWLAND AT THE PLA-MOR ROLLER SKATING RINK, CLEVELAND, photograph by Crawford, 1947. Gift of William Howland, African American Roller Skating Archives Project.

(BELOW) **NATIONAL ROLLER RINK** (Kalorama Road), Washington, D.C., ca 1950. License plate. Gift of Charles Hawkins, African American Roller Skating Archives Project.

(OPPOSITE) **NEW YORK HAND DANCE–STYLE SKATING,** by Hez, ca 1950. Carbon steel candleholder. Our Family Skate Association Collection, African American Roller Skating Archives Project.

DOCUMENTING POLITICAL LEADERSHIP. The Congressional Black Caucus (CBC) was a product of the Black power movement of the 1960s and 1970s. Congressman Charles Diggs of Detroit formed the Democratic Select Committee in 1969. It was a precursor to the CBC, which was organized on June 18, 1971. The CBC provides a means for Black members of the U.S. House of Representatives to exhibit a united leadership front and to work together in addressing common political concerns. It continues to be an influential force on Capitol Hill.

In 1976, the CBC Foundation was established as a research and educational institute, dedicated to furthering political studies and action in the African-American community. The CBC Foundation launched TransAfrica in 1977, an organized lobbying effort on behalf of African policy issues.

PROGRAM, CONGRESSIONAL BLACK CAUCUS FOUNDATION, INC., 18th Annual Legislative Conference, Washington, D.C., September 14-18, 1988. Congressional Black Caucus Foundation, Inc., Papers.

(OPPOSITE) THE DELEGATE (a biographical magazine highlighting persons and organizations who contributed to community advancement), New York, Melpat Associates, 1971. Congressional Black Caucus Foundation, Inc., Papers.

The Struggle Continues

A Look Into The Future

18th Annual Legislative Weekend

September 14-18, 1988 ★ Washington, D.C.

Congressional Black Caucus Foundation, Inc.

cbcf

AFTERWORD

CHARLES L. BLOCKSON

Had it not been for these men and a few women, hundreds of volumes needed today for research would not be in our major collections. Somewhere, there should be a Hall of Fame for these incurable bibliomaniacs. — Dorothy Porter Wesley

THESE ENCOURAGING, THOUGHTFUL WORDS WERE SPOKEN MANY YEARS AGO by my late mentor and friend Dorothy Porter Wesley, whom I call the queen mother of African-American bibliophiles and collectors. During a career at Howard University that spanned 43 years, including many years as curator of the university's Moorland-Spingarn Research Center, Dr. Wesley transformed Howard's collection of Black culture into an internationally known treasure. Probably because she was a collector herself, she displayed a special affection for collectors. She once said that "all the collectors that I have known have indeed been bibliophiles" and "it seems to me that the two words 'collector' and 'bibliophile' are interchangeable."

My own path to collecting books and documents pertaining to African-American history and literature began in a most inauspicious way in my hometown in Norristown, Pennsylvania. When I was in the fifth grade in an integrated classroom during a lesson on American history, after listening to a litany of contributions made by white Americans to our country, I raised my hand and asked my teacher about the notable contributions made by Frederick Douglass, Harriet Tubman, Paul Robeson, Joe Louis, Jesse Owens, Marian Anderson, and several others that I had heard my parents and relatives talk about. My teacher betrayed no hint of uncertainty: "Negroes have no history. They were born to serve white people." Out of the confusion of the moment grew anger so great that I set about deliberately seeking more knowledge about my people. Shortly after the incident with my teacher, my grandfather told me that his father and several other relatives had escaped with Harriet Tubman on the Underground Railroad from Delaware to Canada. Our family is documented in William Still's famous 1872 book *The Underground Railroad*.

Though more than 50 years have passed, I remember the moment when I entered the Moorland-Spingarn Research Center as if it were yesterday. While viewing the magnificent collection of books bound in cloth and vellum that had been collected by bibliophiles like Jesse E. Moorland and Arthur B. Spingarn, a surge of revelation and emotion coursed through my heart and mind.

Enclosed behind the glass bookcases were an abundance of rare items by and about people of African descent I wished for and could not afford to purchase at the time: the writings of Leo Africanus, Juan Latino, Phillis Wheatley, Olaudah Equiano, Jacobus Capitien, Armand Lanusse's *Les Cenelles*, and Benjamin Banneker's *Almanac*. Banneker was an astronomer, mathematician, botanist, and surveyor. As an African American he played an unusual role in surveying the Federal Territory (now Washington, D.C.), our nation's capital.

Recognition, of course, should be given to the writers of the Harlem Renaissance, including the works of Langston Hughes, Zora Neale Hurston, Claude McKay, Countee Cullen, Jessie Fauset, Nella Larsen, W. E. B. Du Bois, James Weldon Johnson, Charles Spurgeon Johnson, and Howard University's distinguished men of letters, Alain Locke and Sterling Brown.

Enclosed in the bookcases were hundreds of other valuable books that had chronicled the lives of African people worldwide. To say that Moorland-Spingarn had a profound impact on me would be to understate its influence, for it prompted me to delve more deeply into Black culture. I became a bibliophile. No longer was I seeking to find a heritage, but to amass a collection to explain a heritage after viewing this endlessly fascinating and voluminous collection. Washington, D.C., had become a mecca for African-American book collectors and bibliophiles starting in the days of Jesse E. Moorland and Daniel A. P. Murray, who worked for the Library of Congress from 1871 to 1923. In 1904, Murray had a list of 5,000 books by and about people of African descent to be included in a massive six-volume *Encyclopedia of the Colored Race* and is largely responsible for establishing the African-American Collection at the Library of Congress. He donated more than 1,400 of his books to the library.

Included among Murray's and Moorland's African-American bibliophile friends were Washingtonians Henry P. Slaughter, John Wesley Cromwell, Carter G. Woodson (better known as the father of African-American History Month), Philadelphian William Carl Bolivar, Cincinnatian Wendell Dabney, and New Yorkers the Rev. Charles Martin and Arturo Alfonso Schomburg, whose name the world-famous Schomburg Center for Research in Black Culture in Harlem bears. These passionate and dedicated bibliophiles and historians, along with Du Bois and others, sponsored annual meetings in Washington, D.C., often meeting at Howard University, to encourage scholarship and to discuss subjects relating to books and other writings pertaining to the African diaspora.

THE LIFE OF A BIBLIOPHILE IS MUCH LIKE THE LIFE OF A GENEALOGIST. It seems to wind and stretch in all directions, like the roots of the venerable old baobab trees in West Africa. Simply put, it is what I am about. My area of collecting is Black literature. The production of literature by people of African descent is rich in tradition. The first substantial collections of Black literature were undoubtedly amassed in the 15th century in the library of the University of Sincere, located in the fabled city of Tombouctou in Mali, West Africa. Knowledge of the cultural center in Timbuktu, and the great libraries in other ancient African cities in Mali, including Djénné and Gao, would come to me later when I started collecting books about ancient and medieval Africa. My early visit to Moorland-Spingarn refined my understanding of Africa dramatically.

In 1983 I was asked to deliver a talk on collecting at the Black Bibliophiles and Collectors Symposium organized by the Moorland-Spingarn Research Center. My topic was entitled Black Giants in Bindings. In addition to bibliophiles and collectors, the conference appealed to historians, librarians, archivists, and researchers and all those interested in collecting, preserving, and disseminating Black history and culture. In 1984 I was commissioned to write an article on the Underground Railroad for the NATIONAL GEOGRAPHIC magazine. The article became the cover story for the July edition of the magazine.

That same year, I donated my personal collection of more than 20,000 items, including books, pamphlets, broadsides, photographs, sheet music, manuscripts, and other items relating to people of African descent, to Temple University in Philadelphia. The Charles L. Blockson Afro-American Collection continues to grow through the acquisitions of both current and retrospective materials numbering more than 150,000 items. Throughout my many years of collecting, preserving, and disseminating knowledge, my longstanding conviction is that no race of people should be deprived of the knowledge of itself. Historical knowledge must be given unto the world to whoever will accept it.

I could not begin to record my life as a bibliophile and curator without paying tribute to the early pioneers who were an integral and knowledgeable part of the Moorland-Spingarn Research Center. The bulk of the collection bears their unmistakable stamp and definitiveness in the variety of historical material related to the African diasporic experience and reflects the words of Dorothy Porter Wesley: "Somewhere, there should be a Hall of Fame for these incurable bibliomaniacs."

(OPPOSITE) **ARTHUR B. SPINGARN COLLECTION OF NEGRO LITERATURE,** bookplate designed by Aaron Douglas, 1920s. Arthur B. Spingarn Papers.

THOMAS C. BATTLE, director of the Moorland-Spingarn Research Center since 1986, is an author, lecturer, and consultant. He is the co-author of *Black Bibliophiles and Collectors: Preservers of Black History* and *Howard in Retrospect: Images of the Capstone.*

ALLISON BLAKELY is a professor of European and comparative history, and the George and Joyce Wein Professor of African-American Studies, at Boston University, as well as being a professor emeritus at Howard University. His books include the award-winning *Russia and the Negro: Blacks in Russian History and Thought.*

CHARLES L. BLOCKSON, curator of the Charles L. Blockson Afro-American Collection at Temple University, is the author of several books, including *The Underground Railroad: First Person Narratives.*

GREG E. CARR is an assistant professor at Howard University, where he has taught in the Department of African-American Studies since 2001. He has researched widely on Pan-Africanism and Africana.

W. PAUL COATES, a former Black Panthers defense captain, served as an African-American studies reference and acquisition librarian at Howard University's Moorland-Spingarn Research Center and is the founder of Black Classics Press.

SPENCER R. CREW is the executive director of the National Underground Railroad Freedom Center in Cincinnati and the former director of the Smithsonian Institution's National Museum of American History. Crew was also a professor of African-American and American history at the University of Maryland Baltimore County and is the author of numerous books.

DE WITT S. DYKES, JR., is a professor of African-American history, U.S. urban history, and gender and family history at Oakland University in Rochester, Minnesota. He is a contributor to such reference works as the *Dictionary of American Biography, Notable Black American Women,* and *Notable Black American Men* and is the co-founder of Detroit's African-American Genealogy Society and the Michigan Black History Network.

JOHN HOPE FRANKLIN is the James B. Duke Professor Emeritus of History and former professor of legal history in the law school at Duke University. He is a recipient of the Presidential Medal of Freedom. His books include the award-winning *From Slavery to Freedom: A History of African Americans.*

DEBRA NEWMAN HAM is a professor of history at Morgan State University. She served as curator of the NAACP Papers at the Library of Congress from 1986 to 1995. She wrote the foreword for *A Colored Woman in a White World,* an autobiography by educator, political activist, and first president of the National Association of Colored Women Mary Church Terrell.

JOSEPH HARRIS is a distinguished professor emeritus of history at Howard University, a lecturer, and an author. He is currently director of the South African Research and Archival Project at Howard University. He has studied the African diaspora extensively and is helping to create a National Slavery Museum in Virginia.

DEIDRE HILL BUTLER is a professor in the Department of Sociology at Union College in Schenectady, New York. Her academic research examines the social geography of race, class, and gender in New England African-American social institutions.

WILLIAM F. HOLTON spent 35 years in the civil service before returning to work at his alma mater, Howard University. Currently, he is conducting oral histories of America's Black Eagles of World War II and is national historian for the Tuskegee Airmen, Inc.

IDA E. JONES is a librarian in the Manuscript Division of the Moorland-Spingarn Research Center. She has taught history at Howard University and the University of Maryland. She is currently writing a biography of educator Kelly Miller.

WILMA KING is the Arvarh E. Strickland Distinguished Professor of African-American History at the University of Missouri-Columbia. King has researched the experiences of free African-American women before the emancipation in 1865 and has written about the experiences of women and children during slavery. She has written, co-written, or edited numerous books, including *Stolen Childhood: Slave Youth in Nineteenth Century America.*

"LITTLE EVA SONG. UNCLE TOM'S GUARDIAN ANGEL," by Whittier and Emilio, 1852. Handkerchief. General Museum Collection.

EDNA MEDFORD is an associate professor, specializing in 19th-century African-American history, and director of graduate studies in the Department of History at Howard University. She was the director for history of New York's African Burial Ground Project and has published more than a dozen articles and book chapters on African Americans, especially during the era of the Civil War.

CLIFFORD L. MUSE, JR., the university archivist at Howard University, is the co-author, with Thomas C. Battle, of the pictorial history of the university, *Howard in Retrospect: Images of the Capstone.* He has taught at Howard University and Catholic University.

JOSEPH P. REIDY's academic specialty is 19th-century U.S. history. Previously an editor with the Freedmen and Southern Society Project at the University of Maryland, he is currently a professor of history and an associate provost at Howard University, where he directs the Black Sailors Research Project. He has published widely on slavery, the Civil War, and slave emancipation in both scholarly and popular journals.

SANDRA G. SHANNON is a professor of African-American literature and criticism at Howard University. She is the author of *The Dramatic Vision of August Wilson* and *August Wilson's Fences: A Reference Guide.* She is co-editor of *August Wilson and Black Aesthetics.*

JEFFREY C. STEWART is a professor of U.S. history at George Mason University in Fairfax, Virginia. His teaching interests include museum studies, comparative slavery, American culture in the 1920s and 1930s, and the history of American thought. Formerly director of research at the Smithsonian Institution's Anacostia Museum, he is the author of a number of books, including *The Critical Temper of Alain Locke.*

ARNOLD H. TAYLOR is an emeritus professor of history at Howard University. His published work includes *Travail and Triumph: Black Life and Culture in the South since the Civil War.*

EMORY JOEL TOLBERT, a professor of history at Howard University, specializes in the history of the United States, African-American history, and the African diaspora. The author of numerous books and artcles, he is also the author of the first regional study of the Marcus Garvey movement, and was senior editor of the *Marcus Garvey and Universal Negro Improvement Association Papers,* Volumes 1–4.

JAMES TURNER is the founder of the Africana Studies and Research Center and a professor of African and African-American politics and social policy at Cornell University. Turner initiated the term "Africana studies" to conceptualize the comprehensive study of the African diaspora. As a Schomburg Research Fellow at the Schomburg Center for Research in Black Culture, Turner conducted research on the political philosophy of Malcolm X that served as the basis for his work on the prize-winning PBS series *Eyes on the Prize.*

RONALD WALTERS, an analyst of African-American politics, is director of the African-American Leadership Institute and Scholar Practitioner Program, Distinguished Leadership Scholar at the James MacGregor Burns Academy of Leadership, and professor of government and politics at the University of Maryland. He is a prolific author, and was awarded the Ralph Bunche Prize for his book *Black Presidential Politics in America.*

DONNA M. WELLS is Prints and Photographs librarian at the Moorland-Spingarn Research Center. She has served as adviser on numerous history-related projects and has published and presented on Washington, D.C., history and on the African-American image.

DEBORAH WILLIS is a professor of photography and imaging and African studies at New York University. She has pursued a career as an art photographer, as one of the nation's leading historians of African-American photography, and as a curator of African-American culture.

CLINT C. WILSON II is a professor of journalism and graduate professor of communications at Howard University. He is also director of the Black Press Institute, a joint project of the National Newspaper Publishers Association Foundation and Howard University. He is the author of a number of books about the relationship between peoples of color and mass media in the United States.

MAX SCHMELING VS. JOE LOUIS FIGHT PROGRAM, June 18, 1936. General Museum Collection.

ACKNOWLEDGMENTS

LEGACY HAS BEEN IN THE MAKING since the Moorland-Spingarn Research Center made its first acquisition. This book could not have happened without the dedication of the staff, our Moorland family.

Thanks and much love to the current staff for their input and for their patience while working on this production: Chief Librarian Jean Currie Church; Curator of Manuscripts Joellen ElBashir; University Archivist Dr. Clifford R. Muse; archivists Dr. Ida E. Jones and Tewodros Abebe; assistants Penny Only, Gladys Toney, Richard Jenkins, and Ishmael Childs; and student assistant Melvin Barolle. A special thanks to Rosa Anthony, administrative officer. The list of former staff at Moorland is too lengthy to mention here, but they formed the foundation of the center's collections. Without your involvement and foresight in shaping the center in its early years and your tenacity in acquiring and building its holdings, Legacy could never have happened.

Ron Ceasar of Ceasar Photography did most of the photography. Ron, your expertise in lighting and your eye for artistry brought the documents, images, and artifacts to life. Your enthusiasm and interest in the project were invigorating. Also thanks to Howard's School of Medicine photographer, Dr. Jeffrey Fearing, who was always available to help with last-minute requests.

Twenty-four wonderful scholars contributed to the writing of this book. Besides the standard criteria that they be experts in their fields, we wanted to use scholars who were familiar with Moorland's resources or with Moorland's role in preserving Black history. Thank you so much for your dedication to the project, in spite of your very busy schedules.

Moorland's mission would be futile without its researchers, particularly Howard faculty, staff, and students. Your writings, exhibitions, films, productions, genealogies, and other projects serve to take the center's rich resources to the rest of the world. To our friends and supporters: Your undying financial and spiritual support has sustained Moorland over the years and has ensured the availability of its resources for future generations. We have to single out Dr. Cynthia Jacobs Carter, the author of *Africana Woman: Her Story Through Time* (National Geographic, 2003), for your encouragement and for introducing us to National Geographic.

Finally, a very special thanks to the *Legacy* team, made up of staff from National Geographic Society's Book Division. You evolved into the dream team. Freelance illustrations editor Susan Blair took our idea and pitched it to executive editor Barbara Brownell Grogan in the fall of 2005. who pitched it to the powers that be at National Geographic. Susan wore many hats, including those of researcher, photographer's assistant, writer, staunch supporter, coach, dream-maker, and friend. Susan Tyler Hitchcock, as editor, helped to ensure that the words also became part of the legacy. Cinda Rose—artist and dream-weaver—worked wonders with the graphics. Laurie Cooper Burns, coordinator for catalogs and promotions, put the initial word out. Although entering late into the project, editor Judith Klein turned out to be someone we couldn't do without. Last, but definitely not least, thank you, Barbara Brownell Grogan, for your belief in the *Legacy* concept and your vitality and enthusiasm in keeping the team excited about the project.

FOUNDERS' PIN BELONGING TO BEULAH E. BURKE, one of the original nine founders of the Alpha Kappa Alpha Sorority at Howard University in 1908. Archives of the Alpha Kappa Alpha Sorority, Inc.

(OPPOSITE) **"MINNEHAHA,"** by Edmonia Lewis, 1869. Marble bust. General Museum Collection.

BIBLIOGRAPHY

Behrendt, Stephen. "Transatlantic Slave Trade," in *Africana: The Encyclopedia of the African and African-American Experience*, Kwame Anthony Appiah and Henry Louis Gates, Jr., eds. (2nd ed.), vol. 5. New York, N.Y.: Oxford University Press, 2005.

Brinch, Boyrereau. *The Blind African Slave, or Memoirs of Boyrereau Brinch, Nick-named Jeffrey Brace. Containing an Account of the Kingdom of Bow-Woo, in the Interior of Africa; with the Climate and Natural Productions, Laws, and Customs Peculiar to That Place. With an Account of His Captivity, Sufferings, Sales, Travels, Emancipation, Conversion to the Christian Religion, Knowledge of the Scriptures, &c. Interspersed with Strictures on Slavery, Speculative Observations on the Qualities of Human Nature, with Quotation from Scripture.* St. Albans, Vt.: Harry Whitney, 1810 (electronic edition available at http://docsouth.unc.edu/neh/brinch/menu.html).

Brown, William Wells. "Narrative of William Wells Brown," in *Puttin' On Ole Massa: The Slave Narratives of Henry Bibb, William Wells Brown, and Solomon Northup*, Gilbert Osofsky, ed. New York N.Y.: Harper, 1969.

Bruns, Roger, ed., *Am I Not a Man and a Brother: The Antislavery Crusade of Revolutionary America, 1688–1788*. New York, N.Y.: Chelsea House Publishing, 1977.

Burns, James MacGregor. *Leadership*. New York, N.Y.: Harper and Row, 1978.

Childs, John Brown. *Leadership, Conflict, and Cooperation in Afro-American Social Thought*. Philadelphia: Temple University Press, 1989.

Chinweizu. *The West and the Rest of Us: White Predators, Black Slavers and the African Elite*. New York, N.Y.: Vintage Press, 1975.

Creel, Margaret Washington. *"A Peculiar People": Slave Religion and Community Culture Among the Gullahs*. New York, N.Y.: New York University Press, 1988.

Cugoano, Ottobah. "Narrative of the Enslavement of Ottobah Cugoano, a Native of Africa; Published by Himself in the Year 1787." In *The Negro's Memorial; or, Abolitionist's Catechism; by an Abolitionist* by Thomas Fisher. London: Printed for the author and sold by Hatchard and Co., 1825 (electronic edition available at http://docsouth.unc.edu/neh/cugoano/menu.html).

Diène, Doudou, ed. *From Chains to Bonds: The Slave Trade Revisited* (Papers from the UNESCO Slave Routes Project). Paris: UNESCO Publishing/Berghahn Books, 1999.

Donnan, Elizabeth. *Documents Illustrative of the History of the Slave Trade to America*, 4 vols. Washington, D.C.: Carnegie Institution, 1930.

Douglass, Frederick. *My Bondage and My Freedom*. New York, N.Y.: Dover, 1969.

Elliot, Jeffrey M., ed., *Black Voices in American Politics*. New York, N.Y.: Harcourt Brace Jovanovich, 1986.

Eltis, David. "The Volume and Direction of the Transatlantic Slave Trade: A Reassessment," *William and Mary Quarterly*, vol. 58, 2001, pp. 17–46.

Franklin, John Hope, and August Meier, eds. *Black Leaders in the Twentieth Century*. Chicago: University of Illinois Press, 1982.

Gaines, Kevin K. *Uplifting the Race: Black Leadership, Politics and Culture in the Twentieth Century*. Chapel Hill: University of North Carolina Press, 1996.

Gordon, Jacob U. *Black Leadership for Social Change*. Westport, Conn: Greenwood Press, 2000.

Hodges, Graham Russell, and Alan Edward Brown, eds. *"Pretends to Be Free": Runaway Slave Advertisements from Colonial and Revolutionary New York and New Jersey*. New York, N.Y.: Garland Publishing, Inc., 1994.

Hofstee, Erik J. W. *The Great Divide: Aspects of the Social History of the Middle Passage in the Trans-Atlantic Slave Trade* (Michigan State University, Ph.D. dissertation), 2001

Inikori, Joseph E. *Africans and the Industrial Revolution in England: A Study in International Trade and Economic Development*. New York, N.Y.: Cambridge University Press, 2002.

———. "The Struggle Against the Transatlantic Slave Trade: The Role of the State," in *Fighting the Slave Trade: West African Strategies*, Sylviane A. Diouf, ed. Athens: Ohio University Press, 2003.

Inikori, Joseph E., and Stanley L. Engerman, eds. *The Atlantic Slave Trade: Effects on Economies, Societies and Peoples in Africa, the Americas, and Europe*. Durham, N.C.: Duke University Press, 1992.

Johnson, Walter, ed. *The Chattel Principle: Internal Slave Trades in the Americas*. New Haven, Conn: Yale University Press, 2005.

Jones, Bryan D., ed, *Leadership and Politics: New Perspectives in Political Science*. Lawrence: University of Kansas Press, 1989.

Klein, Herbert S. *The Atlantic Slave Trade*. New York, N.Y.: Cambridge University Press, 1999.

Lewis, Bernard. *Race and Slavery in the Middle East*. New York, N.Y.: Oxford University Press, 1990.

Mann, Charles C. *1491: New Revelations of the Americas Before Columbus*. New York, N.Y.: Alfred A. Knopf, 2005.

Marmon, Shaun E. *Slavery in the Islamic Middle East*. Princeton, N.J.: Markus Wiener, 1999.

Matson, R. Lynn. "Phillis Wheatley—Soul Sister?" *Phylon*, vol. 33, 1972.

Miers, Suzanne, and Igor Kopytoff. *Slavery in Africa: Historical and Anthropological Perspectives*. Madison: University of Wisconsin Press, 1980.

Palmer, Colin. *Human Cargoes: The British Slave Trade to Spanish America, 1700–1739*. Urbana: University of Illinois Press, 1981.

Phillips, Donald T. *Martin Luther King, Jr. on Leadership: Inspiration and Wisdom for Challenging Times*. New York, N.Y.: Warner Books, Inc., 1999.

Pope-Hennessy, James. *Sins of the Fathers: A Study of the Atlantic Slave Traders, 1441–1807*. London: Weidenfeld and Nicolson, 1967.

Rawick, George P., ed. *The American Slave: A Composite Autobiography*. Westport, Conn.: Greenwood Press, 1972–79.

Richards, Phillip M. "Phillis Wheatley and Literary Americanization," *American Quarterly*, vol. 44, 1992.

Robinson, David. *Muslim Societies in African History*. New York, N.Y.: Cambridge University Press, 2004.

Rodney, Walter. *A History of the Upper Guinea Coast, 1545–1800*. New York, N.Y.: Cambridge University Press, 1970.

———. *How Europe Underdeveloped Africa*. Washington, D.C.: Howard University Press, 1981.

Sampson, Edith. "The Hamitic Hypothesis: Its Origins and Function in Time Perspective," *Journal of African History*, vol. 10, no. 4, 1969.

Sersen, William John. "Stereotypes and Attitudes towards Slaves in Arabic Proverbs: A Preliminary View," in *Slaves and Slavery in Muslim Africa: Islam and the Ideology of Enslavement*, John Ralph Willis, ed. Totowa, N.J.: Frank Cass, 1985.

Taylor, Robert L., and William E. Rosenbach, eds. *Contemporary Issues in Leadership*. Boulder, Colo.: Westview Press, 1993.

Taylor, Susie King. *Reminiscences of My Life in Camp with the 33d United States Colored Troops Late 1st S. C. Volunteers*. Boston: published by the author, 1902 (electronic version available at http://docsouth.unc.edu/neh/taylorsu/menu.html).

Thornton, John K. *Africa and Africans in the Making of the Atlantic World, 1400–1800*. New York, N.Y.: Cambridge University Press, 1998.

———. *Warfare in Atlantic Africa, 1500–1800*. New York, N.Y.: Routledge, 2000.

Walker, Sheila. *African Roots/American Cultures: Africa in the Creation of the Americas*. New York, N.Y.: Rowman & Littlefield Publishers, 2001.

Walters, Ronald W., and Cedric Johnson. *Bibliography of African American Leadership*. Westport, Conn.: Greenwood Press, 2000.

Walters, Ronald W., and Robert C. Smith, *African American Leadership*. Albany: State University of New York Press, 1999.

White, John. *Black Leadership In America: 1895-1968*. New York, N.Y.: Longman, Inc., 1985.

ILLUSTRATIONS

All photographs are courtesy of the Moorland-Spingarn Research Center, Howard University. Additional photographs were taken by Ron Ceasar Photography: pp. 4; 6; 8; 9; 10; 12-13; 16; 20-21; 22 (upper and lower); 23; 24; 25 (all); 26-27 (lower); 28; 29; 30; 31; 38; 39 (upper); 42 (left upper and lower); 43; 55 (upper); 57; 58; p. 64 (all); 68; 70-71; 73 (upper); 75; 76; 77; 80; 86; 101; 102; 106; 107; 108 (left); 109; 116; 119; 122; 132-33; 134; 136 (left); 144; 148; 161 (all); 168; 172; 179; 180; 181 (all); 182 (all); 183; 202 (all); 210; 216; and 219.

Jeffrey John Fearing: pp. 98-9 and 218.

LEGACY
TREASURES
OF BLACK HISTORY

Edited by Thomas C. Battle and Donna M. Wells

Published by the National Geographic Society

John M. Fahey, Jr., *President and Chief Executive Officer*

Gilbert M. Grosvenor, *Chairman of the Board*

Nina D. Hoffman, *Executive Vice President;*
President, Books Publishing Group

Prepared by the Book Division

Kevin Mulroy, *Senior Vice President and Publisher*

Leah Bendavid-Val, *Director of Photography Publishing*
and Illustrations

Marianne R. Koszorus, *Director of Design*

Barbara Brownell Grogan, *Executive Editor*

Elizabeth Newhouse, *Director of Travel Publishing*

Carl Mehler, *Director of Maps*

Staff for this Book

Susan Blair, *Project Editor and Illustrations Editor*

Judith Klein, *Editorial Project Manager*

Susan Tyler Hitchcock, *Text Editor*

Cinda Rose, *Art Director*

Meredith Wilcox, *Administrative Director of Illustrations*

Abby Lepold, *Illustrations Coordinator*

Richard S. Wain, *Production Project Manager*

Sanaa Akkach, *Design Assistant*

Connie D. Binder, *Indexer*

Rebecca Hinds, *Managing Editor*

Gary Colbert, *Production Director*

Manufacturing and Quality Management

Christopher A. Liedel, *Chief Financial Officer*

Phillip L. Schlosser, *Vice President*

John T. Dunn, *Technical Director*

Vincent P. Ryan, *Director*

Chris Brown, *Director*

Maryclare Tracy, *Manager*

Founded in 1888, the National Geographic
Society is one of the largest nonprofit
scientific and educational organizations in
the world. It reaches more than 285 million
people worldwide each month through its
official journal, NATIONAL GEOGRAPHIC, and its
four other magazines; the National Geographic
Channel; television documentaries; radio
programs; films; books; videos and DVDs;
maps; and interactive media. National
Geographic has funded more than 8,000
scientific research projects and supports
an education program combating
geographic illiteracy.

For more information, please call
1-800-NGS LINE (647-5463)
or write to the following address:

National Geographic Society
1145 17th Street N.W.
Washington, D.C. 20036-4688 U.S.A.

Visit us online at
www.nationalgeographic.com/books

For information about special discounts
for bulk purchases, please contact
National Geographic Books Special Sales:
ngspecsales@ngs.org

Library of Congress Cataloging-in-Publication Data
Legacy: treasures of Black history / edited by Thomas C.
Battle and Donna M. Wells; preface by John Hope
Franklin.
    p. cm.
Includes bibliographical references and index.
ISBN-10: 1-4262-0006-4
ISBN-13: 978-1-4262-0006-9
1. Moorland-Spingarn Research Center—Catalogs. 2.
African Americans—History. 3. African Americans—
Social conditions. 4. African Americans—History—
Sources—Catalogs. 5. African Americans—
Historiography. 6. Slavery—United States—History. 7.
United States—Race relations—History. I. Battle,
Thomas C. II. Wells, Donna M. (Donna Marcia), 1953-
E185.53.W3M66 2006
973'.04960730074753—dc22   2006048223

Printed in U.S.A.